NORA V. DAZA

A Culinary Life

Personal Recipe Collection

WITH MICHAELA FENIX

Published and exclusively distributed by
ANVIL PUBLISHING, INC.
3rd Floor Rudgen II Building
17 Shaw Boulevard,
1600 Pasig City, Philippines
Telephones 633-6121/633-6136/631-7048

1st printing, 1992
2nd printing, 1993
3rd printing, January 1994
4th printing, November 1994
5th printing, 1995
6th printing, 1996

Art Direction and Cover design by Delfin M. Pascual
Book Design by Del Pascual and Michaela Fenix
Illustrations by Del Pascual, Ricky Velarde and Brian Afuang

National Library of the Philippines
Cataloguing-in-Publication Data

Recommended entry:

Daza, Nora V.
    A Culinary life : personal recipe
collection / Nora V. Daza ; with
Michaela Fenix. - Pasig, Metro Manila
: Anvil Pub., c1992. - 179 p. : ill.
; 24 cm
    Index: p. 173-179.

    1. Cookery, Filipino. I. Fenix, Michaela.
II. Title.

TX725P5   641.5'09599   1994   P944000008
ISBN 971-27-0212-X

Printed by
Orogem International Publishing Co., Inc.
58 Kalayaan St., Diliman, Quezon City

This book is dedicated to

Bong & Gloria
Sandy & Tessa
Mariles & Eduardo
Stella & Jay
Nina & Louie

PREFACE

THE SEVENTIES started the era of cookbooks. So many have been printed around the world that one shop in San Francisco specializing only in cookbooks is kept viable and well-stocked. Most of the cookbooks on Asian cuisines, however, are by foreign writers. This may be because whatever has been written down is not done in the Roman letters we know (e.g. Chinese characters). Apart from that, the system of measurements used is not the one we have been used to. Sunda Khin, a Burmese friend of my daughter Mariles, told me that even to this day, the amounts of salt and spices in Burma are given in "the size of the tamarind seed" or "the size of a betel nut."

Anyone who has written out a recipe knows how time-consuming and tedious the process can be. For many cooks, knowing the dish is enough and does not necessitate writing the recipe down. And, as in Burma (Myanmar), most cooks hardly use mathematically precise measurements. Cookbook writers in trying to quantify a "dash of pepper" or a "few drops of flavoring" spend hours kitchen-testing in order to approximate the imprecise descriptions.

One motivation that prompts a person to write out a recipe is the desire to duplicate a favored dish or at least someone else's desire to do so. That has always been so for me. Some of the recipes here were given by friends I constantly prodded to reveal how a dish I enjoyed could be recreated. Yet more than just sharing with readers these gems, all the recipes included here are what I think Filipinos should have in their repertoire of Philippine cooking.

As in my previous cookbooks, all recipes here give the real procedures and don't hide anything. I do not believe in giving a modified version of a recipe just so certain portions of it may be kept secret.

I recall how uneasy I felt having to explain to a Western friend about the presence of meat loaf and spaghetti recipes in my first cookbook. That was in 1965 and from then, I resolved to gather only recipes for a "truly Filipino" cookbook. Today, some 27 years after, I have decided that being Filipino doesn't mean disregarding all foreign influences. It means including everything, yes, the food that may have originated somewhere else but have settled here to become an integral part of Filipino fare.

But more than just a collection of recipes, this book has evolved to become something more personal to me. As I wrote introductions to each section and each recipe, I noticed how much I recalled the talks with culinary friends, the times in my grandmother's and aunts' kitchens, and observations and experiences during my travels and stay in foreign countries and in the provinces. It has become a sort of memoir of more than forty years of work with food and people, something that I had been wanting to do for a long time now.

Finally, this book is a tribute to all the other cookbooks that came before and which have inspired me to write my own. My cookbook bibles have been the following:

- *Singalong-San Andres Cookbook,* a collection of family recipes by the women who lived along the Singalong-San Andres areas right after the war compiled by my aunt, Mrs. Mariquita Villanueva Adriano, and Mrs. Rosario Kalaw de Roxas.

- *Recipes of the Philippines* by Enriqueta David Perez, an excellent source by my friend Etang who was food editor of the *Herald*;

- *Joy of Cooking* by Irma S. Rombauer which was later updated with her daughter, Marion Rombauer Becker, a comprehensive book of so many recipes; and

- *Fannie Farmer,* also known as the *Boston Cookbook,* considered the oldest of the genre and which was recommended by my mother-in-law, Angeles Ortega Daza.

I have always had this love affair with cookbooks and was devastated when the majority of my collection was destroyed in a fire which engulfed my living quarters in Ermita. Nothing gives me more pleasure than reading through a recipe and I have this uncanny ability of being able to memorize a recipe right away. I can also usually tell whether the dish will turn out good or bad without having to kitchen-test. Once in a while I have been pleasantly surprised with a recipe I thought would turn out bad. Those occasions only serve to remind me that one never really stops learning especially in the world of cooking.

NORA V. DAZA

W HEN I finally decided that the course I wanted to take in college was Communication Arts, I was told that I was following the footsteps of one of my baptismal ninangs, Nora Villanueva Daza. Even as my mother and my aunts said that, none of them seemed surprised about it.

Nora Daza by then was a famous personality. She was food writer and TV host of a popular cooking show; she had opened a highly-rated French restaurant which branched out to other cities in Metro Manila; she also operated successful restaurants abroad like her own Aux Iles Philippines in Paris and the Maharlika in New York.

I did get to work on television but, unlike my ninang, I was behind the camera, on a desk as copywriter and then once in a while as stage manager for special shows.

Years later when I changed medium, from television to print, I was asked to write about food and then after that, I was expected to keep on writing about it. Armed only with appreciation for good food and always insecure about not knowing much about cooking, I wrote every week for a magazine. Contrary to most people's impressions, food writing is not always a pleasant experience and having to do it on a regular basis makes it almost tedious. And more than the eating, the best times have been talking with people who either are into the food business or are just food lovers.

One of those times was interviewing Nora Daza in 1988. The article was entitled "Is there life after Au Bon Vivant?" and while it asked about the fate of her French restaurant in deteriorating Ermita, at that time the only one left among her restaurants, it also asked what her plans were. She had said then that she felt she had already done enough and that she wanted to retire and maybe write about her life.

She wrote from Paris after that thanking me for the article, a rather depressing letter that seemed to say "good-bye, I am retiring but not gladly." And when Au Bon Vivant closed shortly after that, I took that as her final exit from the culinary scene.

It was a surprise to see her name just a few months after as a partner in a new Thai restaurant, Mai Thai in Pasig. Not long after, she called to ask help about this new cookbook she wanted to write. And she thought it a great idea for us to work together.

This is my first cookbook and in the beginning, I felt daunted by the prospect. But Nora Daza, who has written perhaps the most successful cookbook here, had so many ideas that needed to be organized and written. That was to be my main work.

The concept changed drastically midway but it was for the better. As it has turned out, the recipes presented here are very personal to Nora Daza and as such, it has become unlike any other cookbook because only she could have written it. Whatever contribution to the text I have done were taken from my own researches during the course of writing my food articles and which she insisted I add to her text. They are few compared to Nora Daza's, and what she has here is but a small portion of her vast culinary experiences. Even with that, I am glad that I coaxed her into remembering some of them and finally putting those down.

MICHAELA FENIX

CONTENTS

This book would not have been finished but for the many people who helped us with it: Lorna Lelis and Elsa Ching Patriarca who compiled, typed, phoned and looked for missing recipes; Neny Regino who translated the Spanish recipes; Del Pascual for the cover design, illustrations and the computer layout, Ricky Velarde and Brian Afuang for the other illustrations; Margie Mendiola and Girlie Pineda for the initial proofreading and correction of text onscreen.

MY
FIRST
RECIPE
·················

M Y EARLIEST appreciation of good food I can trace back to my walks with my father, Alejandro J. Villanueva. Sometimes it would be at dawn when we would go to a Chinese vegetable garden and gather bunches of lettuce and green onions which we would make into a salad later. Other times it would be a walk to the bakery while the morning was still dark and we would wait for the bread to be brown, all the while inhaling the delicious aroma of baking bread.

I do remember other times shared with him—when I used to sip from his cup of fresh milk in the morning or just watched him prepare roast lamb with such ceremony.

When Food became my profession, Papa would ask me to sample doughnuts he had made or a pudding or a chicken dish. He would even try out some recipes from my cookbook and some demonstrated on my television show.

Villanueva Pancakes

By the time I was eight, I had acquired some skill in cooking, particularly in baking muffins and producing pancakes. A neighbor, Mr. and Mrs. Leon Guinto Jr. had mah-jong parties a few afternoons a week. I used to volunteer myself to prepare the merienda.

I learned to relish the pleasure of receiving praise for my cooking that early because my pancakes were light but thick in size and tasty. The recipe came from my mother, Encarnacion Guanzon de Villanueva. It was she who also taught me how to make my first adobo, sinigang, escabeche, cocido, butterscotch pie, cream puff and Pampango frozen fruit salad.)

The twist in this recipe is that we had a small frying pan just for this recipe. I would pour the batter until it was almost 3/4 thick. Then I would wait until the pancake rose and bubbles appeared on the top. I would then flip it and finish my cooking.

a six-inch frying pan (heavy metal pan is recommended)
1 1/4 cups all-purpose flour
3 tsp. baking powder
1/4 tsp. salt
4 eggs, separate yolk and egg white
1 1/4 cups milk
1/4 cup melted butter
1 tsp. vanilla

Sift flour, baking powder and salt into a large bowl.

In another container, mix 4 egg yolks, milk and melted butter. Blend the liquid mixture into the flour mixture until a smooth batter is formed.

In another bowl, beat egg whites until stiff but not dry and fold this into the batter in the large bowl. (To save time, start to heat your pan before you beat the egg whites. Use only a medium flame.)

The pan is just right for cooking when you sprinkle drops of water into it and it sizzles. Pour the batter until it is about 3/4 inch thick and the batter touches the sides of the pan. The pancake will rise. It is ready to be turned over when bubbles start appearing especially on the sides. Flip over and cook the other side. Peep to see if the pancake is golden brown. When it is, remove from pan. Serve with butter and maple-flavored syrup.

Home-made syrup
1 cup white sugar
1 cup brown sugar
1 cup water
1 tsp. maple flavoring

Stir the sugars and water to dissolve the crystals slightly. Allow the mixture to boil. Do not stir once the syrup is formed. Just drop in the flavoring and tilt the pan to mix the flavoring. Serve.

* Should you want to prepare the syrup and then keep for future use, add 1/4 cup corn syrup to the sugars. This will prevent the sugars from forming crystals.

Storing eggs

It is better to store eggs with the tapered end down. (See figures below). The idea is to create a bigger distance for the yolk from the air pocket at its wider end. This is because the yolk is richer than the white and hence more perishable. Storing eggs the proper way will make these last longer.

When buying eggs by the dozen, store these in the refrigerator still in their cartons and put them in the back part of the refrigerator. Placing eggs at their designated place at the refrigerator door does not help in their storage life. The less eggs are jarred, the longer they keep. Storing temperature of eggs is about 30 to 31°F.

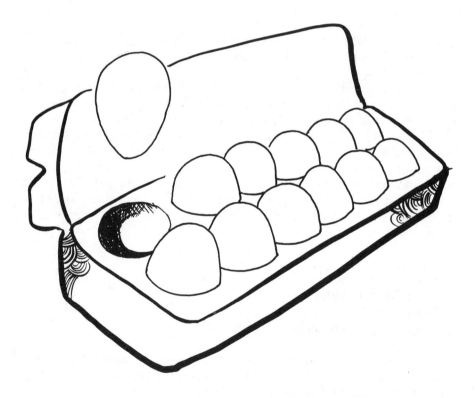

APPETIZER

PORK BARBECUE

KUHOL BICOL

CRISP SPINACH LEAVES

VIETNAMESE SPRING ROLLS

UKOY

PINSEC FRITO ❏ FRIED WONTON

STUFFED MUSSELS

MUSSELS MARINIER

SISIG

WHETHER THEY are called *canapes*, hors d' oeuvres, *antipasto or antipasti, nibblers or nosh they are all bits of tasty food that are meant to stimulate the appetite and prime one's sense to enjoy the main* plat de resistance.

Today's appetizers are also used to calm the hungry while awaiting the other guests or the meal that will be the main attraction of the lunch or dinner.

When choosing appetizers, one should select those that balance the flavors or contrast with the dishes that are to come. If the main dish is focused on meats or fish, hors d' oeuvres *should be vegetable that can be used to dunk, spear or pick up with fingers into a tasty dip with cream, yogurt or cheese.*

With the world of food crossing national boundaries as never before, appetizers can go from fried wontons, lumpia, ukoy, *crispy spinach leaves to cucumbers, carrots and celery dunked in a dip with innumerable variations.*

In Manila where almost all Filipinos come to spend some time during the year, those who have traveled and lived abroad come back and serve appetizers and meals they have learned and adapted all over the world. Food in Manila now features those found in the United States, Europe, the Middle East, Hongkong and Singapore.

Pork barbecue

Elsa Ching Patriarca is a lady I have had the good fortune to know. She comes from Pagsanjan, a tourist town in Luzon which boasts of a ride in the rapids as its main attraction. Recently, Sylvia Cancio Lim, my partner at the Mai Thai restaurant and I with members of our family were invited to celebrate Elsa's birthday in Pagsanjan. The luncheon spread was an absolute delight. Elsa was busy getting all the details of the various meals perfect and couldn't do the barbecue herself. So she gave her recipe for the **pork barbecue** *to a neighbor. We found the barbecue already excellent but Elsa's mother, a formidable cook herself, felt that Elsa's "timpla" (marinade mixture) was far superior to what we just had. I have had to coax Elsa to share her secret. Here it is:*

1 kilo pork, cut into bite-size pieces

Marinade:
1/3 cup *calamansi* **juice**
3/4 cup soy sauce
3/4 cup Seven-Up™
1 1/2 tbsp. chili sauce
3 tbsp. sugar
1 tsp. msg
Salt & pepper to taste

Pork pieces must be marinated overnight in a refrigerator. Arrange in barbecue sticks. Mix marinade with banana catsup*. Brush on pork pieces and broil over charcoal.

*****UFC™ Banana Catsup** -use with marinade to brush barbecue as it is being charcoal broiled

Kuhol Bicol

Not many years back, kuhol *(snails, or* escargot*) became a hit in Manila. The initial enthusiasm has died down. Yet,* kuhol *is a delicious, inexpensive source of protein.* **Kuhol Bicol** *was a crowd drawer at the Aux Iles Philippines restaurant in Paris. The French, being lovers of escargot, took to this recipe with gusto.*

This recipe was given to me by Cely Kalaw, owner of the Grove, a restaurant that pioneered in serving a daily buffet of Filipino dishes.

---

2 tbsp. cooking oil
1/3 to 1/2 cup *bagoong alamang*
4 cloves garlic, chopped
1 thumb-size fresh ginger,
    chopped
1 thumb size fresh turmeric
    (*luyang dilaw*), chopped
1 cup chopped onions
3 kilos *kuhol*
1 to 2 pcs. finger pepper
    (Jalapeña)
5 cups coconut milk
2 cups coconut cream
* For spicy hot *kuhol* add 1 to 3
    pcs. hot chilis

Wash river snails thoroughly, scrubbing the shells. Heat cooking oil and add garlic sauteeing till golden brown. Add ginger, turmeric, onions and cook till mushy. Add *bagoong* and cook until all are well-blended. Add *kuhol* and five cups of coconut milk. Cook over low heat tightly covered until kuhol is tender. Add coconut cream and continue cooking till sauce is thick and oil comes to the surface. If mixture should dry out, add water and continue cooking. *Kuhol* should be tender before it can be served.

Crisp Spinach Leaves

*When **Crisp Spinach Leaves** first appeared in the Manila food scene, the dish received rave notices. The enthusiasm has waned a bit because of repeated servings. Yet this is still a star offering in many cocktails, so here it is.*

Select fresh, large and unblemished spinach leaves.

Prepare a tempura-like batter using:
1 cup cold water
1 large egg
1 cup sifted cake flour

Beat egg with water and add flour all at once. Mix lightly, stirring not more than five times. Lumps will remain but this is all right. A pinch of salt may be added to improve the flavor of the batter.

Tempura Dipping Sauce:

1 1/2 cups of *Dashi-no-moto* (Japanese instant soup stock)
1/2 cup soy sauce
1/4 cup *Mirin* (sweet sake, a Japanese wine)
Combine the above ingredients; bring to a boil and cool.

When serving Crisp Spinach Leaves, you can add some grated white radish and *wasabe* (Japanese green mustard) in mounds on the side.
Prepare the *wasabe* mixture by adding drops of water to 2 tsp. of *wasabe* powder. Mix, adding water till a smooth paste or medium consistency is attained.
Grate white radish and arrange in a mound. The *wasabe* may be put in tiny mounds also. The blend of the **Tempura Dipping Sauce** with the grated radish and *wasabe* is usually served for Tempura.

Vietnamese Spring Rolls

In the 1930s and earlier, fried lumpia *was filled with either an assortment of vegetables or ground beef and pork with cubed potatoes. Today,* fried lumpia *in all its variations can be found all over the whole world but it is certain that it is Chinese in origin. The Chinese say "Popia" for* lumpia. *Most countries in Southeast Asia use a name that is derived from "Popia."*

I find the Vietnamese version which is called Cha-do *very good. It is served with fresh vegetables and has more ingredients for the filling than other versions.*

300 gms. crab meat
8 medium sized shrimps cut into strips
2/3 cup ground pork
1/2 cup soy bean noodles, (bean thread)
2 pcs. Chinese mushrooms (soaked in water for 1 hour), sliced very thinly
1 egg
1/2 of a big onion, chopped
White part of green onion
Salt and pepper
Patis (fish sauce)
Rice paper (wrapper)

Sauce:
3 tbsp. *patis*
Garlic
Hot Chili
6 tsp. vinegar
6 tsp. water
5 tsp. sugar
carrots, sliced thinly in fine strips
white raddish, sliced thinly in fine strips

Mix all ingredients together and wrap in rice paper (*lumpia* wrapper) firmly. Fry in oil. Care should be taken that the oil is not too hot so that the ingredients inside the spring roll will cook properly. Store the lumpia upright so that the excess oil can be drained.

For the sauce: Mix all ingredients.

Serve with very fresh lettuce, basil leaves, mint leaves and coriander leaves (*wansuey*), and the sauce.

Ukoy

The origin of **ukoy** *may be lost to us. I know that it was a native* kakanin *(native cake) sometimes sold by food vendors in baskets which they carried on their heads. It uses the same batter as* maruya *(banana fritters), both made with rice flour, but while* maruya *is sweet,* ukoy *is salty.*

Today, ukoy *is more sophisticated and served in the best restaurants. The new recipe borrows from the Japanese tempura and the batter is now lighter and the* ukoy *cooked crispier. The* sawsawan *(dipping sauce) is a mixture of vinegar, salt, and chopped or crushed garlic and black pepper.*

1 cup small shrimps
1 egg
1 cup water
3/4 cup cornstarch added to
1/4 cup all-purpose flour
1 tsp. baking powder
1/4 tsp. baking soda
1 tsp. salt
1/2 teaspoon *patis*
dash msg
oil for deep frying

Wash and clean shrimps thoroughly. Drain and set aside.

Beat egg slightly then add water, cornstarch mixture, baking powder, baking soda, salt, *patis*, msg, and shrimps. Stir to mix.

Heat oil in a wok or skillet. Drop about 2 tbsp. of the mixture and fry until golden brown and crisp. Dry on absorbent paper. Serve with vinegar and garlic sauce.

Pinsec Frito/ Fried Wanton

A variation of the Filipino fried lumpia *is* **Pinsec** **Frito** *or* **Fried** **Wanton**. *The filling used is the same. The dish is a regular* dim sum *entrée. It may be served either steamed or fried.*

1/2 kilo ground pork
1/4 kilo fresh shrimps, chopped
4 stalks spring onions, chopped
1 piece canned bamboo shoots, chopped, about 1/2 cup
2 to 3 pieces dried Chinese mushroom, soaked and chopped
1 tbsp. soy sauce
1 egg
2 tbsp. cornstarch
salt and pepper
dash of sesame oil
oil for deep fat frying
50 pieces *wanton* wrappers*

Mix all ingredients except the oil for frying and the *wanton* wrappers. Fry a small piece to check on seasoning. Put bits of the mixture, the size of a thumb's nail and fold. Have cooking oil not too hot because raw pork has to be allowed to cook at the same time the *wanton* is expanding. Cook *wanton* mixture for about 1 1/2 to 2 minutes. Serve at once with sweet sour sauce.

Sweet Sour Sauce:
1/4 cup vinegar
1/4 cup sugar
1/4 tsp. salt
1/2 cup pork stock
2 tsp. cornstarch
1 tbsp. water in which cornstarch is dispersed
1 tbsp. cooking oil
2 tbsp. tomato catsup

Combine vinegar, sugar, salt and stock. Bring to a boil. Add dispersed cornstarch to mixture. Allow to thicken. Fry tomato catsup and add to the vinegar mixture. Some sliced long hot peppers may be added.

Stuffed Mussels

Mussels or tahong *are very often cooked in one of these two ways—baked in garlic butter or as soup as a kind of chowder. I am sharing my version of those two ways of cooking here.*

1 kilo mussels
1 cup butter
2 to 3 cloves of garlic, chopped finely
Salt and pepper
Sprig of parsley, chopped finely

Soak mussels in water to allow sand to be spit out.

Boil a minimum amount of water together with chopped onions seasoned with salt and pepper. Cook until mussels just open. Set aside to cool.

Cream butter so that garlic and chopped parsley can be incorporated into the butter mixture. Season with salt and pepper.

Place mussel on one shell and cover the mussel with the butter mixture. The mussels can then be arranged on a tray, sealed with foil and refrigerated. It can be baked just before being served.

Before serving, bake the stuffed mussels uncovered in an oven at 350°F. The butter will melt and a film with the garlic and parsley mixture will settle on top of the mussels. Serve immediately. A bed of sliced lettuce or cabbage can serve to dress up this appetizer of seafood course.

* A variation is the addition of some grated cheese on top of the mussels before baking.

Moules Mariniere

In France, this is one of the best ways to serve mussels. It uses white wine thus making it a festive fare rather than an everyday dish. This recipe is a perfect blend of flavors that brings out just the right acidity of wine and the pungent uniqueness of the shallots or native onions.

1 kilo mussels
3/4 cup chopped shallots (*sibuyas tagalog*)
1 sprig fresh parsley, chopped
salt and freshly ground black or white pepper
1 cup white wine
1 bay leaf (*laurel*)
1/2 tsp. thyme
2 heaping tbsp. of butter

Clean mussels thoroughly and allow to soak in water to allow sand to be spit out. Place the cleaned mussels into a large stockpot and add the rest of the ingredients. Cover tightly and allow the liquid to boil. Simmer for about 8 minutes just until the mussels open. Serve immediately.

* There is no need to add water for the juice of the mussels will blend with the white wine. Correct salt if needed.

** I sometimes add some fresh cream to give it a richer flavor. Another variation is the addition of just a little curry or some chili.

Sisig

Sisig must be the safest food to eat because it is cooked three times over; first boiled, then charcoal broiled, then cut up and mixed with spices after which it is further cooked on a sizzling plate toasting some of the bits in the process.
Sisig is a Pampango invention but no one really knows who started it.

The best place to have sisig *is along the outdoor eateries by the railway in Angeles City each one claiming to be the "orig.". Service starts only at sundown and one can choose from several stalls (about 35) all curiously bearing women's names.*

*Other railroad track delights include sticks of what Angeleños call "barbecued spare parts" because the pieces are made of pig's ears and cheeks (with "*ahit pogi*" quality because there were no stray hair) and chicken's ass (also called "elevator" because it opens and closes) and the neck. MF*

This recipe was provided by Gloria de la Paz, the former food assistant of my television show, Cooking it up with Nora. *She now works at the Safari Lodge, Leonard Wood Rd. in Baguio City. She learned this recipe from her mother who is Pampangueña and who was also a good cook.*

1/2 kilo pig's ears (today pig's cheeks are also included)
salt and bay leaves (*laurel*)
1 cup chopped onions
freshly ground pepper
2 to 3 tbsp. native vinegar
1.4 tsp. msg
1 to 2 pcs. small chilis (hot chili)
100 grams pork or chicken liver (broiled)

The pig's ears should be throughly cleaned with salt and vinegar and plenty of water. Boil till tender in water, salt and bay leaves. Water should completely cover the pig's ears. When ears are tender, broil over charcoal.

Remove all bones and see that all portions are chopped in even sizes. If not to be served right away, the chopped pieces can be frozen.

Before serving, measure the amount to be served and chop equivalent amount of fresh onions. (e.g. 1 cup of chopped pieces of pig's ears equals 1 cup of chopped onions). Season with vinegar, salt, pepper, hot chilis and vetsin (msg). Add broiled pork or chicken liver and chop in pieces the same size as the pig's ears.

Wedding Breakfast Soufflé

Once at the Maharlika Restaurant in New York City, we were retained to serve 150 very important bankers for lunch. But I was in Manila at the time and so I went to see then Central Bank Governor Gregorio Licaros to tell him that I would leave for New York and personally supervise the event.

It was fortunate that I went. On the menu was Cheese-Spinach Soufflé for 150 persons! Not only did we not have enough ovens to bake this amount, we also had the kitchens at the basement while the dining room was on the fourth or fifth floor. And that kind of soufflé has to be served right away straight from the oven. The lunch would have been a disaster. We barely had time to scrap the soufflé from the menu and substitute something else.

This recipe though is different. The dish can be prepared the night before and after the soufflé is baked, the air does not escape immediately since the cheese and starch from the bread keeps the air in and the souffle can stand for some time without sagging.

This is one quick and elegant way to serve breakfast to a group since the recipe contains many items one takes at breakfast. It is a unique way to serve about 16 to 20 pesons with just fruit or salad on the side.

12-15 slices bread, trimmed and cubed (enough to cover the bottom of the Pyrex baking dish)
1 1/4 cups *chitcharo* or brocolli
2 cups shredded Cheddar cheese (8 ounces)
2 cups ham, cut into cubes
6 eggs, slightly beaten
2 cups milk
1/2 cup cream
1 finely chopped onion
1 teaspoon dry mustard or 1 tablespoon prepared mustard
1 Pyrex baking pan 9 x 13 inches

Cover bottom of buttered 9 x 13-inch baking pan with half of bread cubes. Arrange vegetables, ham and cheese over bread; top with remaing bread cubes. Combine eggs, milk, cream, onion and mustard; pour over bread and other ingredients. Seal with plastic sheet and refrigerate for several hours or over night. Bake uncovered in a 350°F oven or until knife inserted in center comes out clean (about 55 to 60 minutes). Let stand 10 to 15 minutes before serving. Cut into squares.

SOUP

LOMO GUISADO
CHICKEN BINAKOL
PESANG MANOK
TOM YUM GOONG
CABBAGE ROSE SOUP
SINIGANG NA HIPON
SPICY CHICKEN SOUP (SOTOAYAM)

W HEN I opened my Philippine restaurant in Paris in 1972, I was surprised to find that the more sophisticated Parisians did not begin their menus with soup. They either had mushrooms or quiche or other light entrees. The reasons for this, I was told, was that soup was associated with either being sick or being a part of the farming community, very rural for the urban Parisian taste.

Today, however, due to pressures of work and time, one dish meals are coming back to Paris so that stews and soups are regaining their status.

For Filipinos, soup can be served as starter or as the main dish. More often, it is one of the many viands served all at the same time which a Filipino diner is accustomed to. I remember that in Paris, whenever a Pinoy customer would eat in the restaurant, the waiters would instruct the kitchen with "sabay bagsak," meaning, all entrees should be served at the same time.

Lomo Guisado

In 1950, when I married into the Daza family, my mother-in-law, Angeles Ortega de Daza was very active in the kitchen. She began preparing our Sunday luncheons on Wednesday. Every Sunday we had a different menu. Most of the dishes were Spanish in origin and she would point out to me how Doña Luisa Lichauco, her cooking teacher at the Centro Escolar would emphasize this or that precaution to take.

One Sunday, we had a soupy meat dish that I had never sampled before. It was **Lomo Guisado***. I immediately asked her the recipe and experimented and tested it until I got it just right. I included* Lomo Guisado *recipe in my cookbook in its second edition. I am told that* Lomo Guisado *originated in the Visayas where they use carabao meat instead of beef and that sometimes, fresh blood would be added to the soup.*

Very important in the preparation of the Lomo Guisado *is the pressing of the meat strips against the side of the saucepan so that the meat juices are squeezed out and dissolved into the broth. The stock therefore attains a very rich flavor and the meat becomes tender.*

---

1 kilo beef tenderloin or round steak cut into 2" strips
3 tbsp. cooking oil
5 segments garlic, minced
2 onions chopped finely
thin strips of ginger
4 big ripe tomatoes, chopped
1/4 cup soy sauce
salt and pepper
4-6 cups beef stock or beef bouillon

Heat fat in a saucepan. Saute garlic until brown. Add onion, ginger and tomatoes and cook over slow fire for 10 minutes. Add meat and soy sauce. Add beef stock 1/2 cup at a time and simmer until meat is done and tender. Add just enough liquid to cover meat strips. Serve hot.

*Beef bouillon may be prepared with 1 cup water for every cube of bouillon.

Chicken Binakol

Chicken Binakol *is a stew that I imagine the kings and princes of the pre-Spanish times enjoyed. Bamboo was abundant everywhere then; herbs, spices and young coconuts were thriving in our islands. It would be natural for people then to prepare this dish.*

I would like to point out as a culinary tip that the young coconut is best added last. When I first tried this dish, the green bamboo tubes were put into a pot of boiling water. This cooked the chicken and allowed the flavor of the bamboo to blend with the stock. However, if fresh bamboo is not available, cooking in a pot will do. It will be less fragrant, but it has become an acceptable Binakol.

This can be served as a first course, but one can use this as a main dish as well.

---

3 cloves garlic, chopped
1 thumbsized ginger, pounded
2 tbsp. cooking oil
1 medium sized onion, sliced
1 stalk *tanglad* (lemon grass) cut into 3 inch pieces
1 chicken (about 1 1/2 kilo) cut into pieces
2-3 tsp. *patis* (fish sauce) to taste
dash of white pepper
1/2 tsp. monosodium glutamate
4 cups rice washing
1 *pandan* leaf, knotted
1 cup grated *buko* (young coconut)
2 cups *buko* water
sili leaves
1 tbsp. spring onion
1 fresh bamboo tube (12 ins. long, 4 ins. diameter)

Saute garlic and ginger in hot oil until golden brown. Add onion and *tanglad*. Add chicken pieces; season with *patis*, pepper and monosodium glutamate. Cover and allow flavors to be absorbed about 6-8 minutes. Add rice washing and *pandan* leaf and cover until meat is tender.

Take out meat and discard all bones. Put back meat in boiling stock. Add *buko* water. Continue for 3 minutes. Add *buko* meat, *sili* leaves and spring onion.

Place mixture in green bamboo and cover with *pandan* leaves and put in moderate oven 350°F for 20 minutes to allow the stew to absorb the flavor of the fresh bamboo. Serve hot.

Pesang Manok

The preparation of Chicken Tinola *and* **Pesang Manok** *are very similar. The difference is in what is added to each soup. Instead of the green papaya found in* Tinola, *pieces of quartered potatoes are added to the* Pesa. *Some may add very little garlic and the pronounced flavor will come from the ginger. These prominence of either the ginger flavor or the garlic flavor in the* Tinola *or the* Pesa *is a matter of choice.*

This comparatively bland soup of Pesa *makes a very good accompaniment with crisp* lechon *and its rich liver sauce. The fat-free* Pesa *balances off the fat-rich* lechon.

1. whole chicken about 1 1/2 kilos
6 cups water
1 piece ginger, the size of a thumb up to the palm
4 - 5 pieces of peeled potatoes cut in quarters
8 - 10 cabbage leaves
1 tbsp. *patis*
1/2 tsp. whole black pepper corn
salt to taste

Cut chicken in serving pieces. Wash into running water to eliminate any broth bones. Place into a deep saucepan and add the water. (Bigger chickens need more eater). Drop in ginger, *patis*, black pepper corn and salt. Boil the chicken until it is half tender.

Add the potato quarters to the cooking pot. Allow the potatoes to be almost cooked and then add the cabbage leaves.* Continue cooking until the cabbage is wilted. Serve hot. With *lechon*, this recipe can serve from 6 to 8 persons.

* Some like to parboil the cabbage in salted water before adding these to the *Pesa*. You may do so if you want to avoid the sulfur aroma in cabbage from mixing with the *pesa*.

Tom Yum Goong
(Thai Hot and Sour Prawn Soup)

My interest in Thai cuisine dates back to the first time I visited Thailand. This was in the early Fifties. Bangkok looked like one of our provincial towns. A friend took me to the wet market to sample Thai cooking and I remember that I didn't like it much. It was something like Pancit Mami, *only sweetish.*

My next encounter with Thai cooking was when I began to appreciate the cuisine. When the Thai ambassador to the Philippines was H.E. Sompongse Faichampa. Madame Vimol Faichampa, the ambassador's wife, arranged a cooking demonstration in her home in North Forbes Park. Her garden included rows and rows of herbs—basil, pandan and lemon grass. What she was specially proud of were the Makrood trees dotting the boundaries of the well-kept and wisely used property.

Finally, it was Urai Meejul who gave me my first lessons in Thai cooking including the world famous Tom Yum Goong *(Hot and Sour Shrimp soup) and* Gaeng Ped Gai *(Curried Chciken). These two dishes complement each other because the stock used in the soup comes from bones discarded from the curried chicken.*

Much of my knowledge of Thai cuisine comes from the efforts of Malulee Pinsuvana. It was she who wrote one of the first Thai cookbooks to be published in English. I met her in 1968 in Jakarta, Indonesia. Ms. Pinsuvana recorded and translated recipes from her native Thai which was not easy to do because their alphabet is different from the alphabet much of the Western world uses. She is one of the pioneers who introduced Thai cooking that is now the rage all over the world.

---

400 g. (14 oz.) medium-size prawns
3 stalks lemon grass
2 cloves garlic
2 tsp. chopped coriander root
4 - 6 pcs. peppercorn
1/2 inch (15 mm) knob fresh *Kha* (Siamese ginger)
2 fresh red chilies
4 small fresh green chilies
6 1/2 c. chicken stock
4 Khaffir lime leaves (Makrood)
1/3 cup vegetable oil

2 tbsp. fish sauce (*patis*)
2 tbsp. lime sauce (*dayap*)
Freshly shredded coriander leaves

Shell and devein the prawns, leaving the tails intact. Retain the heads and shells. Cut the lemon grass into short lengths, approximately 1 inch and pound lightly with the back of the knife. Place the garlic, coriander root and peppercorn in a mortar and pound into a smooth paste. Slice the ginger, cut the chilies into very tiny rings and shred the lime leaves. Heat the oil in the sauce pan, add the prawn heads and shells and stir-fry for 3-4 minutes. Then add chicken stock and bring to a boil. Cover the pan, reduce the heat and simmer for 10 minutes. Pour the stock through a fine strainer into a fresh saucepan and bring back to the boil. Stir in the spice-paste and add the lemon grass, ginger, lime leaves and prawns. Bring back to boil and allow to cook for approximately 3 more minutes.

Bulalo

Every Filipino restaurant in Manila now carries **Bulalo**. But this dish broke into the food scene only in the late 70s and early 80s. It began in Santo Tomas, Batangas when Emilia Robles Carpio opened her eating place at the "Crossing," the junction between the provinces of Laguna and Batangas, where she cooked her "*Nilagang Bias*" in a "*balde*" or sometimes in a kersone can. In those days, a serving of *Nilagang Bias ng Baka* cost 60 centavos. A kilo of bias cost P3.50.

In 1971, Emilia Carpio moved her growing business into a bigger lot and charged 90 centavos per serving. The name, however, was changed as one customer baptized the dish as "*Bulalo*" which means *tuhod* or knee. The bulalo cut has a lot of tendons and ligaments and is cooked till every bit of the meat is tender with the connecting ligaments already gelatinous. Because of the popularity of the *bulalo*, finding this particular cut of beef is no longer easy or inexpensive.

Emilia's daughter Conchita Carpio Ascana and her daughters, Rosy and Grace, have continued the thriving eatery that now features an assortment of other Filipino favorites such as *Rellenong Talong, Sinaing na Merlia* wrapped in banana leaves, *Menudo, Bulanglang na Gulay, Morcon, Mechado,* and of course, *Bulalo* and *Bulalo* steak.

Bulalo is proudly Filipino and has become a part of most Philippine restaurants. Don :Amado Alba, a Spaniard who has made Manila his home, has invented his own version of the *Bulalo.* He called it "*Batok-Tuhod*" using the neck cut of the beef as well.

Cabbage Rose Soup

The **Cabbage Rose Soup** *is in my other cookbooks (as Cabbage Roll Soup) but I feel that it hasn't been fully appreciated. Nor have I seen it served in many of the homes I have been invited to for dinner. Yet, it is certainly a party dish, slightly more tedious to prepare but this can be an impressive first course.*

The thing is, one must have a Chinese soup bowl so that the "lumpia"-like pieces can be arranged fitting snuggly at the bottom. The green cabbage leaves will look like rose petals and the strips of ham and egg will add color to the "flower." Over that, the chicken soup is added that is transparent so that the decor underneath is clearly seen.

I learned this recipe from a Chinese lady whose name escapes me now. Let me entice you to try this soup, a recipe which I rewrote because the procedures in my older cookbooks were not very clear.

1 cup cooked chicken meat
1/2 cup cooked pork
3/4 cup *apulid* or water chestnut, chopped
1/2 cup cooked ham, chopped
1 egg white
1 tbsp. cornstarch
1 1/2 tbsp. onion, chopped
2 eggs plus 1 egg yolk with salt scrambled then cut in long thin strips
4 slices cooked ham, in long thin strips
5 cups hot chicken broth
14 large cabbage leaves.
Salt to taste.

Chop chicken and pork meat to a paste. Blend in water chestnuts and ham. Add egg white and cornstarch, onion and salt. Blend well.

Parboil cabbage leaves. Remove the midrib. On each piece of prepared cabbage leaf, spread 2 tbsp. of mixture. Arrange ham and egg both in long strips at the center and roll as you would *lumpia Shanghai*. Steam the filled and rolled cabbage for about 15 minutes. Use any steamer with just water at the bottom of the pan.

Cut the cooked rolled cabbage into 1 1/2 inch pieces. Arrange this compactly at the bottom of the Chinese soup bowl to make it appear like a rose. Individual bowls are easier to do.

Heat the chicken broth. Clarify by adding beaten egg whites and clean egg shells. Boil broth with the egg whites and egg shells. It is the albumin in the egg white that coagulates with the particles in suspension in the stock that is easily strained out after the soup is allowed to boil. Strain by pouring the stock through a clean, dampened cheese cloth or a fine strainer.

Pour the clarified chicken stock slowly in the bowl. Season with salt and serve. Makes 5 servings.

Sinigang na Hipon

Sinigang *is an Asian soup that can be found in Burma, Malaysia, Indonesia and Thailand. In the Philippines, it is a favorite. We make* sinigang *with seafood—fish, shrimps or prawns—and meat such as beef and/or pork. Traditionally, fish and shrimp* sinigang *stock is made with rice washing. This seems to be a Filipino trait for I have not seen this done in Indonesian or Malaysian cookbooks. I know that our cooks at the* Mai Thai *restaurant do not use rice washing.*

To give our soup the sour bite that is typical of sinigang, *we use green tamarind or camias or green tomatoes. Sometimes a twist of* calamansi *can bring the soup up to the desired acidity. In Iloilo and Negros,* batuan *which grows wild is used to sour their* sinigang.

When making sinigang *with meat, I like to season the soup before I add the meat or seafood so that the flavor seeps into the chunks of meat or the pieces of seafood. If tubers are added to beef or pork, care is taken so that the tubers are done by the time the meat is sufficiently tender. Leafy vegetables are added last.*

Sinigang *with lots of vegetables is a good dish to serve for those on a diet or those with little time. Last minute preparation are really minimal.*

---

2 tbsp. oil
1 onion sliced
3 - 4 pcs. half-ripe tomatoes, chopped (about 1/2 cup)
8 - 10 pcs. *camias*
6 cups rice washing
200 gms. fresh shrimps, (medium-size)
1 tsp. salt
2 cups *kangkong* (swamp cabbage) leaves and tender stalks

Saute onion and tomatoes. Add the *camias* and cook until tender and mushy. Add the rice water. Let boil. When boiling, drop the shrimps. Season with salt. Add *kangkong* and cook 2 minutes

* Instead of shrimps, fish may be substituted such as *lapu-lapu, apahap, talakitok.* Other vegetable substitutes are *mustasa* (mustard leaves), *sitaw* and *sigadillas. Calamansi* or green *sampaloc* (tamarind) can also be used to sour the soup.

Spicy Chicken Soup
(Soto ayam)

Soups are very popular in Malaysia, and the Malays generally serve them with the main meal. Alternatively, you can convert a soup into a meal in itself by adding noodles to it. To this soup, you can add scalded rice vermicelli (bihon), hard cooked quail's eggs and tailed beansprout.

2 cups water
chicken (1.8 kilogams), cleaned and cut at the joints
2 tbsp. cooking oil
2 medium carrots, boiled and mashed
salt and pepper to taste
1 large onion, finely sliced and deep fried for garnishing
2 spring onions, finely chopped, for garnishing
lemon wedges

Grind the following ingredients together:

2 tbsp. black peppercorns
1/4 cup *bagoong alamang*
1 thumb-size *luyang dilaw* (turmeric)
8 shallots or 2 medium-size onions
1 thumbsize piece fresh ginger
4 cloves garlic
5 candlenuts or 10 almonds
1 stalk lemon grass (use white part only)

Boil the chicken in water. Simmer until cooked. Remove chicken. Strain the stock and keep it on a gentle simmer until stock is reduced to half its volume.

Heat the oil in a frying pan and stir in the ground ingredients until fragrant. Add the cooked fried ingredients to the stock. Mix in mashed carrots and chicken. Cook for 5 more minutes. Correct the seasoning. Serve hot with deep fried onion flakes, spring onions and lemon wedges.

Fish Curry
Nga-myin si-pyan

Sunda Khin is Burmese and I met her ages ago in Paris. She became a close friend of my daughter, Mariles and when she and her husband Wes moved to Manila, our friendship deepened. My family and friends have enjoyed her Burmese dishes over the past years and visits always include talks about the culture in our respective countries and those of our neighbors—Thailand, Malaysia and Indonesia.

I am including some choice recipes of Sunda Khin with ingredients that are not only available here but are also common items. The recipes also give us some clues about the style of cooking in Khin's country as well as in other Asian countries.

---

1 kilo fillet of fish (lapu-lapu or any white fish)
1/4 tsp. turmeric powder
1/2 tsp. shrimp paste (*bagoong*)
1/4 tsp. salt
3 tbsp. fish sauce (*patis*)
1/2 cup oil
1 cup onions, chopped or minced
2 cloves garlic, crushed
1 tsp. ginger, crushed
1 tbsp. paprika powder
1/2 tsp. chili powder (or crushed dried red chili)
1 tbsp. tamarind paste (thick tamarind juice)
6 coriander sprigs
1/2 cup water (optional)

Marinate the fish fillet (cut into desired pieces) with turmeric, shrimp paste, salt, fish sauce and set aside.

In a large pan heat the oil and when the oil is hot, turn down heat and brown the onions, garlic, and ginger until soft. Mix well. Add paprika and chili powders. Stir and immediately add the marinated fish fillet. Stir lightly and cover. Shake the pan frequently and cook for about 15 to 20 minutes. Add the tamarind paste/juice and water (optional) and the coriander. Turn off heat. Check the seasoning and correct if necessary before serving.

Beef Stewed in Cinnamon Sticks

1/2 kilo beef, cut into cubes (stew meat)
2 tbsp. cooking oil
1 cup onions, diced
2 cloves garlic, crushed
2 pcs. bayleaf (*laurel*)
1 tsp. paprika
2 pcs. cinnamon sticks
salt to taste

Marinade:
1/2 tsp. turmeric powder
2 slices ginger, minced
1 tbsp. soy sauce
2 tbsp. *patis* (fish sauce)

Marinate meat for 4 hours or overnight.

Heat oil. Saute onions, garlic and bayleaf. Add paprika and cinnamon. Add meat and marinade. Stir well till meat turns brown. Cover, turn down heat and simmer for about 30 minutes. Stir and cook for another 20 minutes or until beef is tender. Correct seasoning. Serve with rice.

Fish with Coconut Cream wrapped in banana leaf

1/4 kilo white fresh fish fillet, cut into pieces
1 tsp. ginger, crushed and finely chopped
1 large onion, chopped
1/4 tsp. turmeric
1 tsp. paprika
1 tsp. oil
1/4 tsp. salt
1 tbsp. *patis* (fish sauce)
1/4 cup thick coconut milk
banana leaf
toothpicks
steamer

Mix all the spices with the thick coconut milk in a bowl.

Divide the fish into 5 portions. Place each portion in a banana leaf big enough to hold it. Fold the banana leaf like an envelop leaving one flap open. Pour the spices and coconut milk mixture into the leaf, then close the open flap and seal with a toothpick.

Place the sealed banana leaves (5 in all) in a steamer. Steam for about 15 minutes. Serve hot with rice.

FISH

GRILLED BLUE MARLIN

BANGUS SARDINE

FISH CARDILLO

FISH KINILAW

PESANG ISDA AND MISO SAUCE

SHRIMP LAING

PESCADO AL HORNO

F OR ME, one of the most authoritative article on fish found in the
Philippines was one written in the 1920s by Albert W.C.T. Herre,
then chief of the Division of Fisheries in the Bureau of Science. Most of
his observations in "Some desirable fishes in the Manila market" printed
in the book **Culinary Arts in the Tropics, Circa 1922** remain the
same to this day. Because he calls fish varieties by their local names, he
has made it easier for the Filipino reader. Not only does Herre give tips
on how and what seafood can be bought in the wet market but also how
to cook fish properly.

Lapu-lapu, even then, was a popular fish and Herre observed that
"unfortunately for the housewife... there are at least seven or eight
different kinds of lapu-lapu." The apahap was also a favorite but, as it is
today, unreasonably priced. He considers banak "surpassed by very few
in delicacy of flavor" but prefers the pompano of Southern California
and the West Indies which he says are of "superlative quality" compared
to that of the local pompano but which he acknowledges as "nevertheless
very good." Herre also chides his fellow Americans who will not try dalag
just because it is called mudfish but he knows that "when served with it
at a hotel or some select dinner party, they eat and enjoy it as long as
they don't know what it is."

Two very good advice from Herre still holds today: "A dead crab is a
dangerous crab" and that "it is probably unsafe to use oysters gathered
in the vicinity of Manila on the eastern shores of the Bay [because it is]
generally too polluted."

Grilled Blue Marlin

It used to be that only small to medium-sized fishes were eaten by the elite in Dipolog City in Zamboanga del Norte. Huge fishes like the sailfish and the blue-marlin were for the masa. *Today, the most prized fish is one of the bigger fish, the blue marlin, especially its tail and fins, considered delicacies when poached and served with drinks.*

Jose "Butch" Bustalino of Dipolog belonged to a group who called themselves "Jokers and the Merry Squires." His and other groups spent afternoons taking tasty bits of blue marlin fins and tail which are gelatinous and tasty.

Butch and his friends set up a restaurant specializing in Dipolog specialities and called it Nandau. *It was there where they also introduced the blue marlin delicacy. Demand was so great that when the tails and fins ran out, Butch Bustalino sliced the flesh as steaks and found that the demand still continued.*

Butch advises that the fish should weigh over 40 kilos so the layer of fat all over the fish gives that desired flavor and tenderness. The blue marlin has an outer covering that is spiny and is removed. The second layer is the skin that one sees as part of the blue marlin steak.

The buyer at wet markets should be careful because some venders pass off the sailfish, which has flesh that is tough and tasteless, as the more expensive blue marlin.

Steaks of blue marlin are broiled over live coals, each side for three to five minutes. *Calamansi* and salt are brushed over the steak. A sauce made of a mixture of *patis*, vinegar, garlic (just a hint) and slices of hot pepper is offered.

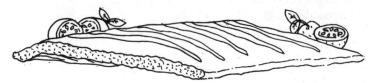

Pan-Fried Blue Marlin

Fry blue marlin in about 2 to 3 tbsp. of butter and season with salt and pepper. Cooking methods used with salmon will do nicely with blue marlin.

Bangus Sardine

When I began to be known as a cooking afficionada, I would get invited to lunches and dinners by people who loved cooking and were good at it. One such person was the colorful Manila mayor Arsenio H. Lacson whose home was on Governor Forbes, the street now renamed after him. I remember Luchi Lacson, his wife, and their little girl named Bingo.

The mayor had a space off their living room which was his private kitchen. It was there where he concocted his dishes. I guess it was where he perfected his now famous **Bangus Sardine**.

I learned about bangus sardine 30 years ago from Oscar Santos of Pampanga and Manila when he demonstrated how to cook the dish on my cooking show. He gave credit for it to Rosie Osmeña Valencia who in turn learned the recipe from Mayor Arsenio Lacson.

Nisena Ortiz de Roces told me that the bangus sardine is something that Iloilo has had for ages. Each family has its own secret recipe but that the Lacsons were reputed to have the best.

My own family have had their own version of bangus sardine. My aunt, Mrs. Emilia Villanueva de Lapus, used to make her own because her brother, Dr. Jose Villanueva, a renowned obstretician and gynecologist, used to love it.

A pressure cooker (size about 4 quarts)
1 kilo *bangus* (20 to 30 pcs. to a kilo is about the right size)
4 pcs. hot chili peppers (*siling pasiti*)
1/2 cup sweet mixed pickles
1/2 cup green olives
2 cups olive oil
1/2 cup soy sauce
3/4 cup brandy or rum
1 tsp. salt
1 tsp. msg
1 pc. bay leaf (*laurel*)

Clean *bangus* without removing scales. Place rack into the pressure cooker and arrange *bangus* in layers. Pour in the rest of the ingredients. Cover pressure cooker and allow mixture to boil until a steady stream of steam flows out of the vent. Place pressure control on vent and allow to cook under pressure for one hour. Allow to cool before removing *bangus* from cooker. *Bangus* will be easier to handle. Entire *bangus* should be edible and is delicious as *hor d'oeuvre* or served with rice.

Fish Cardillo

This fish dish is simple to prepare but is surprisingly tasty. It is really just fried fish with a saute of garlic, onions and fresh tomatoes to which is added some stock and beaten egg. Very often, a dish such as this is forgotten and then when one makes it again, one rediscovers that it is quite good, tasty and inexpensive.

No one knows the origins of **fish cardillo**. *I suppose that someone must have gotten tired of plain fried fish and decided to add sauce. During the* Great Maya Cookfest Culinary Exchange Program, *it was thought good enough to merit being demonstrated to our Asian neighbors.*

1 kilo whole fish (or fish steak), cleaned
1 tsp. salt
cooking oil for frying
2 cloves garlic, crushed
2 medium-sized onions, diced (3/4 cup)
2 pcs. medium-sized tomatoes, diced (1 cup)
2 pcs. eggs, slightly beaten
1 cup water
salt and pepper to taste

Clean fish; cut crosswise into serving pieces if desired or leave whole. Salt and set aside.

Heat oil and fry fish until nicely browned; drain and set aside in a platter.

Pour excess oil and leave some to saute garlic, onion and tomatoes until soft. Add seasonings and water. Bring to boil; remove from heat and stir in beaten eggs.

Pour mixture over fried fish; serve hot.

Fish Kinilaw

Kinilaw na isda *is basically raw fish salad. What makes the standard* kinilaw *different from the Japanese* sashimi *is that the raw fish is almost "cooked" by the vinegar that is used to soak the fish for a while before being squeezed out. Finely chopped ginger and onions are usually added, spiked with hot chili and flavored with* calamansi *and salt.*

Variations, however, are many. Coconut milk is sometimes added for some fish like the tanguigue *not only for a richer quality but also to take out the fishy taste. Some people prefer toasted shredded coconut meat with their* kinilaw. *A Davao version is very plain* bariles *(large tuna) fillet that uses a minimum of vinegar and so maintains its raw red color.*

And then there are those who like their kinilaw *with mayonnaise. This variation seems to take rather seriously the American definition of raw fish salad. But done by an expert, the result is one that blends well the sour taste from the vinegar and the sweet taste of the mayonnaise.* **MF**

---

1 kilo white meat fish (tuna, *labahita* or *bangus*)
skinned and deboned
1/2 cup vinear
1 thumbsized ginger root, cut into fine strips
1 cup onions, chopped
1/2 cup tomatoes, seeded and chopped
1/4 cup green onions, chopped
1/2 cup vinegar
1 - 2 tsp.salt
2 - 4 small hot chilis, pounded
1/2 cup *dayap* juice or *calamansi* juice
1/2 - 3/4 cup coconut cream

Wash the skinned fish and cut into bite-sized pieces. Add 1/2 cup vinegar to rinse and gently wash the fish pieces in vinegar. Squeeze vinegar out. Add ginger, onions, tomatoes, green onions, 1/2 cup vinegar, salt and chilis. The amount of chilis will determine how "hot" your *kinilaw* will be. Add the 1/2 cup *dayap* juice or *calamansi*. The dayap gives a better flavor than *calamansi*. Add salt and allow the marinated fish to "cook" in a covered bowl in the refrigerator. Correct seasoning. The fish flesh will turn white. Just before serving add the coconut cream, and serve at once.

Variation:

1/2 kilo fresh fish (tuna, *tangigue*, *labahita* or *bangus*), skinned and deboned
3/4 cup lime or *calamansi* juice
1 medium-sized onion, diced
1 medium-sized tomato, peeled, seeded and diced
3 tbsp. olive oil (optional)
4 pcs. *jalapena* pepper, seeded and sliced into thin strips
1 small ginger, finely chopped
salt and pepper to taste

Garnishings:
lettuce leaves
lime slices
parsley leaves

Slice meat of fish into serving pieces and place in glass or ceramic bowl. Pour lime juice and toss gently. Cover and refrigerate for at least an hour.

Add the rest of the ingredients and stir gently to blend. Refrigerate until ready to serve.

Arrange on lettuce leaves and garnish with lime slices and parsley leaves.

Courtesy of the Maya Kitchen Culinary Arts Center, Liberty Flour Mills.

Pesang Isda and Miso sauce

Pesang Isda *would be a dish that very early Filipinos prepared for their families.* Pesa *flavors consist mainly of ginger and rice water* (hugas bigas). *Without rice water, the* pesa *will not be up to par. Fresh fish and vegetables are also musts.*

The addition of the **miso sauce** *is a strong Chinese influence but the dish is distinctly Filipino.*

---

2 medium-sized fresh fish (*dalag*, *lapu-lapu*, *carpa* or
apahap) about 400 gms. each
2 cups rice water (*hugas bigas*)
salt to taste
2 tbsp. oil
2 cloves garlic, chopped
1 2-inch piece ginger, crushed
1 medium-sized onion, quartered
2 bunches *pechay*
2 stalks green onions, chopped
fish sauce (*patis*) and msg to taste

Miso sauce:
1 tbsp. cooking oil
2 cloves garlic, crushed
1 small onion, chopped
4 pcs. tomatoes, chopped
2 tsps. *miso*
salt to taste

Clean and cut fish into serving pieces. Season with salt. Set aside.

In hot oil, saute garlic until golden brown. Add in ginger and onion and cook until tender. Stir in the fish and the rice water. Boil for 2 minutes. Add the peppercorn and pechay and green onions. Continue cooking until vegetables are tender. Avoid over-cooking the fish and vegetables.

Prepare the *Miso* sauce.

Saute garlic in oil until brown. Add the onions and tomatoes. Cook for 3 minutes, then add *miso* and mash mixture. Add 2 tablespoons fish stock (from pesa stock) and cook 3 minutes more. Season with salt.

Shrimp Laing

Laing *is a dish that originates from Bicol. In large sections of the wet markets in both Naga and Legaspi, one sees all kinds of gabi leaves, stalks and roots that are the major ingredients in* laing.

Of all cuisines found in the Philippines, cooking in the Bicol region is the one which most resembles those found in Malaysia and Indonesia. The use of spices for the majority of the hot foods found here, the use of coconut milk and certain vegetables, and the bagoong *they use which is closest to the* blachan *of Malaysia and Indonesia support my conjectures.*

I first tasted Laing *as a child when it was cooked by our laundry girl. She used* tinapa *(smoked fish) as filling and I found it very exotic probably because it tasted so different from what we then had at home. Now this dish is a favorite of many.*

1/2 kilo shrimps, chopped finely
2 small young coconuts, grated
1 onion, chopped
1 tsp. salt
10 - 15 pcs. wilted *gabi* leaves
1 cup thin coconut milk
2 pcs. *siling labuyo* or hot pepper

Combine shrimps, coconut and onion. Season with salt. Chop. Wrap by tablespoons in *gabi* leaves. Arrange in an earthenware pot and pour thin coconut milk over wrapped mixture. Cover and simmer over low flame, shaking pot once in a while to avoid burning. When almost done, add the thick coconut milk and *sili*. Continue cooking until sauce thickens.

Pescado al Horno

This is a fish dish which I consider one of the best. Unfortunately, I no longer remember who shared this recipe with me. It was probably one of the dishes that was taught at the Manila Gas Cooking School *in the late 1950s. It was during that time when I was made director of the cooking school when I really sharpened my cooking skills. As I have often heard it said, "To get to know something well, teach it!"*

I have rewritten this recipe so it will be easier to follow. I also recommend that you cook this in a dish you can serve at the table.

---

1 fresh *lapu-lapu* or *bacoco*, about 800 grams to a kilo
1/4 kilo medium-sized fresh shrimp

Marinade:
1/4 cup *calamansi* juice
1 tsp. salt
1 tsp. pepper
1/4 tsp. paprika

Have fish thoroughly cleaned and shell shrimps leaving the tail intact. Let fish and shrimps soak in the marinade for at least 20 minutes.

Prepare stuffing:

Stuffing:
1 red sweet pepper (bell pepper) - cut into strips
1 onion, sliced
1 - 2 tsp. sugar
1 tsp. salt

1/4 tsp. paprika
1/2 tsp. msg

Combine all the stuffing ingredients and insert into the stomach cavity of the fish. Coat fish and shrimps with 1/4 cup of bread crumbs.

Arrange breaded fish and shrimps on a baking sheet. Prepare the following ingredients:

1 cup olive oil
1 cup tomato sauce
1 onion sliced in rings
1/2 red bell pepper cut into strips
1/2 cup bread crumbs
1/2 cup grated cheese (parmesan, dry cheddar cheese or *queso de bola*)

Pour olive oil and tomato sauce over fish and shrimps. Garnish with onion rings and red pepper strips. Sprinkle generously with bread crumbs and cheese.

Bake at 350 degrees F. for about 45 minutes or until the fish is done. Baste occasionally. Serve right in the baking dish for the sauce that has stuck to the dish is delicious. Garnish with sprigs of parsley and serve hot.

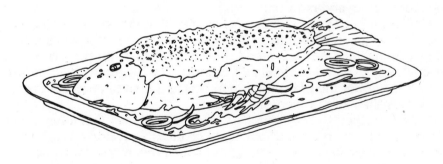

Palengke

One of the best features of wet markets is that requests such as custom-made cuts are always granted. *Bangus* can be cut *daing*-style, sliced for *sinigang* or turned inside out for deboning for *relleno*. There is no need to ask the *hito* vendor to whack the live catfish on the head and clean it because it is *de rigueur*. But at the Calamba market, they still ask in earthy Tagalog: "*Yayariin ko na ba?*"

Vendors have also learned a thing or two about advertising. They know how to attract buyers with *karatolas* that say their *lapu-lapu* and *talakitok* are "genuine," the *hito* and *tilapia* are "native" and the chico is "Peñeras." They show the superiority of their wares by indicating the sources: Batangas beef, Lucena *tanguigue*, Bonoan *bangus* and Bataan *alimango*. You cannot be sure if what they claim is true unless you really know by sight and smell what the produce should look like.

Years of marketing, however, have taught me some tell-tale signs. For instance, Bonoan *bangus* can never be large, has a smaller head and one tail fin is longer than the other. If the vendor says the fish is *maliputo*, be wary. *Maliputo* hardly reaches the market because it is a rare fish caught only in Taal lake and any supply is soon gobbled up by buyers in the area or by specialty restaurants. Some venders also pass off *malasugue* as blue marlin but the former has reddish meat and tough skin while the latter has white meat and thin skin. The *malasugue* is just as delicious charcoal-broiled but is not as expensive as the more tender and rarer blue marlin.

Market tricks to hoodwink buyers are many. It may be as simple as using red or green reflectors on lights to enhance the color especially of fish. Sometimes they rub blood (from other fishes) on fish that is not freshly caught (*ilado*) to simulate freshness. The biggest trick at Muñoz market is to print the price in big numbers and then underneath that the words "half kilo" in very small letters.

But the market is not all that bad. Your *suki* will tell you if her wares are not that fresh and will even extend credit. If you shop enough in one place, sometimes you get to know your *suki*'s whole family and know the life history of each. You can even get a *bayong* for Christmas. It is also surprising that some never forget your face even if they don't know your name. Others may address you with a respectful *ate* or *kuya* or the more familiar "*dar-leeng*." Still others make your day with their comments. One *castañas* vendor at the *talipapa* on Carvajal St. in Binondo said: "*Kung may sira sabihin niyo lang at dadalhin natin sa Mental hospital.*" **MF**

MEAT

CHICKEN RELLENO
CRISP ADOBO FLAKES
CHICKEN AND PORK ADOBO
ADOBONG MANOK SA GATA
BATANGAS ADOBO
BISTEK FILIPINO
HUMBA ❑ DINUGUAN
CALLOS
CRISPY PATA
DELICIOUS HAMBURGER
MORCON
CALDERETTA
KARE-KARE
LENGUA ESTOFADA
PAELLA
PASTEL DE LENGUA
PINATISANG MANOK
MENUDO
COCIDO
PUCHERO FILIPINO

V ERY EARLY writings note that goats, carabaos and deer were the meats our ancestors hunted and ate. Pork may have come from the wild boar, the "baboy damo" or jabali as the Spanish called it.

In my childhood days, pigs were almost all black with an occasional albino. They were small with long snouts. A dear neighbor, Carolina Marino Guerra taught me that the better breed was one that had a short snout and with limbs that were muscled even when it was young.

Today, what we have are cross-bred pigs that are best suited for our climate and yield excellent pork. In fact, pork is the one item in today's markets that we can be proud of.

From the 1980s, the pork and poultry industries had big companies investing millions to produce the meats most popular in the Philippines. It is cattle, however, that has not been cultivated enough to meet the demands of today's Filipinos.

Today, the quality of pork has improved, making it more tender probably due to the better distribution of fat in the meat. Chicken, on the other hand, has become bland and less tasty than those which were grown and marketed up to the 1950s. Ducks and geese are still not available in steady quantities. Pigeon raising was quite common in most homes all over the Philippines but this practice seems to have decreased considerably. Quails are raised mostly for eggs which are in demand in Chinese restaurants. Among the sources of meat, it is cattle that seems to have been introduced later in our history.

Beef has undergone changes in marketing and concepts through the years. It was believed that good beef had fat that was yellow. This was usually associated with Batangas beef, then and now still synonymous to high quality local beef. I was also under the impression that beef in the country is different from those found abroad.

Those impressions, however, were corrected by Mr. Gerry Arañez, a specialist who fattens cattle in his own farm in Batangas for his stores in Metro Manila. From him I learned that yellow fat comes from cows that are past calf-bearing stage and are then slaughtered for beef. Good beef should be cherry red in color and the fat should be white. And from what Mr. Arañez has been producing in his farm, we know that quality beef comparable to that raised in Kobe, Japan, can be had here.

Œ Œ Œ

My own recollections about the cattle industry starts in Batangas. My grandmother would give each of her grandchildren calves as one of her Christmas gifts. These were distributed to various farmers in the area who would feed and fatten the calves for us. This was known as the "iwi" system. When the cattle was ready for market, the price it fetched would be divided between the farmer and the one who gave him the calf for fattening. Perhaps since the farmer had a stake in the cattle, care was better. This may be one of the reasons why beef in Batangas is of superior quality.

I remember my grandmother telling Isabelita, my sister (now Mrs. Pablo Malixi) and I, how many heads of cattle we had that year. I vaguely remember that a head of cattle fetched something like P25 then. I would think how much richer my sister was than me because she was older and consequently had more heads of cattle than I did.

Œ Œ Œ

The process of ageing the meat is something relatively recent. Until frozen cuts were introduced in our groceries, the Filipino buyer would insist on having his beef fresh from the slaughterhouse. This must have been because the quality of freshness, such as in fish, was associated with not having food chilled or frozen beforehand.

I remember that in the late 1960s, I was invited to join a group of French restaurant and hotel owners who were going to attend the "Hotel Show" in New York City. We were quite a big group and I remember distinctly that for the three official dinners where we were invited—at the New York Hotel Association in one hotel, at Hyde Park and at Cornell University at Ithaca—we had the same main dish served to us, Roast Beef. I guessed that the Americans knew about the critical nature of the French and did not want to take chances and so served what they thought was one dish which they could not go wrong. I also doubt if they ever learned that they had all served the same main dish. The French, to their credit, never mentioned this fact. We never talked about it. What we discussed was how they loved the flavor and tenderness of the Roast beef. What we argued about was the freshness of the beef.

During that time, the French never practiced ageing beef and, because of the good quality beef served to us, they were all insistent that the beef served was what they called "fresh." Since I graduated from Cornell University at least ten years earlier, I knew how cattle was slaughtered and marketed in the United States and that Americans always aged their beef. But no one would believe me. I challenged them with bets. They accepted, but I was never able to convince them I was right.

Cattle in France is slaughtered in their abattoirs and one can see sides of beef being brought into meat shops still bloody. In the famous restaurant Pied de Cochon in Les Halles, beef vendors with their bloody aprons sit elbow to elbow with the bejeweled customers partaking of the famous "Onion soup gratinee."

Chicken Relleno

One of the best **Chicken Rellenos** *I have ever tasted was in the home of Dr. and Mrs. Agustin Liboro. They had a family cook who was called Mang Bero, at that time already bent with age, but whose relleno was excellent. When Mang Bero cooked relleno, it was like a ritual and he produced beautifully browned chicken every time. To order, one had to give a lead time of about two weeks. Mang Bero considered his specialty a trade secret and I tried to duplicate it in this recipe.*

A most prized advice on cooking the stuffing was given to me by Mrs. Rosita Ocampo de Fernandez whose family is also known for good cooking. She said to half-cook the stuffing in butter in order to cut down the chances of food poisoning. The result is as good and is certainly much safer.

1 large chicken (about 1 1/2 to 2 kilos)
3 tbsp. soy sauce
3 tbsp. *calamansi* or lemon juice
1/2 kilo ground pork
1/4 kilo cooked ham, chopped finely
4 pcs. vienna sausage, chopped finely
1/4 cup sweet pickle relish
3 eggs
1/2 cup grated cheese
10 pcs. green olives, pitted then chopped
1/2 cup raisins
1 - 2 tbsp. tomato catsup
salt and pepper to taste
1 tbsp. msg
2 hard boiled eggs, quartered
1/4 cup butter

Debone chicken for stuffing. Marinate in soy sauce and *calamansi* juice. Set aside.

Mix thoroughly next 11 ingredients. Fry about a tablespoon of the mixture. Correct seasonings. Stuff chicken, arrange quartered eggs in the center. Sew up opening and wrap in aluminum foil. Bake in moderate oven (350°F) for 1 1/2 hours.

When almost done, unwrap and continue baking until chicken is brown. Baste with butter occasionally. Cool and slice. Arrange in a platter.

Serve with gravy and Glazed Sweet *Camotes*. Serve 12.

Gravy:

Chicken liver, gizzard and heart
3/4 cup pan drippings
3 tbsp. flour
2 cups broth
salt
1/4 tsp. pepper
1 tsp. msg

Boil chicken gibblets in 2 1/2 cups water. Reduce to 2 cups. Chop gibblets, set aside. Heat pan drippings, blend in flour and brown slightly. Add chopped giblets, pour in broth stirring constantly. Cook until thick. Taste and correct seasonings. Serve with stuffed chicken.

Adobo

From family vignettes, I know that we had pork **adobo** that was stored in Chinese jars with a thick layer of pork fat to seal the *adobo*. The jars were then kept in the *banggerahan*, the wash basin in old style kitchens that had wooden slats for drying plates and glasses.

Pork *adobo* is cooked in a mixture of vinegar, salt, garlic and peppercorn. Over the years, chicken was added to the pork and so was bay leaf (*laurel*) and soy sauce to give not only color but add flavor as well. The soy sauce was also a substitute for salt although some still put salt with the sauce.

Pork *adobo* not only keeps well but tastes better when allowed to age in pork fat. It was probably prepared for the sailors who plied the long Manila-Mexico galleon routes from the 17th to the 19th centuries. This must explain the surprising find I made in one California super-market. There was a prepared seasoning for Mexican *adobo* stew. When I tried it, I found that it was similar to our own except that it had more *achuete* and chili was added.

When I first lived in Paris and was testing recipes to be included in the Aux Iles Philip-pines menu, I decided to use pork chops for the adobo instead of the usual pork cubes to reduce the fat and sticky sauce which usually turn off foreigners. Chicken was also cut into well-shaped pieces instead of the random way that is usual in our cooking.

Filipinos, however, look for the mass of browned meat swimming in pork fat. Many still enjoy sauteeing the pork fat with garlic which are then added to cooked rice for the delicious *sinangag* (fried rice).

I have often asked myself what makes *adobo* a Filipino favorite. Apart from being a reliable stand-by food, it must also be the taste, the description of which I accidentally discovered when I prepared *adobo* in Paris one winter. Instead of storing the dish in the refrigerator, I left it in the oven. A few days after that, the dish had developed a distinct aroma and conse-quently the taste I had assiduously tried to evolve in Paris, a slightly rancid taste. When I told this to a Western lady, she shivered in disgust. I should have asked her what she thought of cheese and wine. These are, after all, products of fermented food.

Crisp Adobo Flakes

If you have served a plate of nicely browned adobo, *you will notice that the portions that have brown crisp sides are picked up first. This recipe from* Via Mare's Glenda Rosales Barretto *makes the entire* adobo *dish crisp. She says that the dish probably originated in Cebu where she learned in one of her visits that Don Sergio Osmeña enjoyed his* adobo *in crisp flakes. Taking her cue from there, Glenda prepared her usual chicken and* pork adobo *and then cooked it until it was dry. Then she flaked the meat and fried it until it was crisp.*

Crisp adobo flakes *is served at Glenda's other restaurant,* Neilson Tower, *as a side dish to her* Kare-kare.

---

1 1/2 kilo chicken
1 kilo pork
1 cup native vinegar
5 tbsp. soy sauce
1 tsp. ground pepper
2 tbsp. garlic

Cut chicken and pork into large cubes and marinate in vinegar, soy sauce, pepper and garlic for at least six hours.

In a sauce pan, stew pork with the marinade for 20 minutes, then add chicken and continue to stew for another 23 minutes. When tender, separate the sauce and meat and let cool. Reduce sauce by cooking in open sauce pan.

Flake the pork and chicken meat and sprinkle sauce over the flakes and mix well.

Fry chicken and pork flakes in pork fat in a wok or deep frying pan over medium heat until crisp and brown, but not burnt.

Serve with sauce in separate container.

Chicken and Pork Adobo

1 cup vinegar
1 head garlic, crushed
10 pcs. peppercorn, crushed
1 bay leaf
2 tbsp. rock salt
4 tbsp. soy sauce
1 kilo chicken, cut int serving pieces
1/2 kilo pork, cut into 1-inch by 2-inch pieces
1/8 kilo pork liver, cut into 1-inch by 2-inchpieces
1 1/2 - 2 cups water cooking oil for frying

In a saucepan, combine vinegar, garlic, crushed peppercorn, bay leaf, rock salt and soy sauce. Put in chicken, pork and liver. Let soak for 30 minutes to 1 hour. Add water and simmer uncovered until tender. Strain sauce; set aside. Take the liver from the meats and chop finely. Combine with the sauce; set aside.

Heat cooking oil and brown garlic and meat pieces. Pour sauce with liver. Stir once, cover and simmer until sauce thickens.

Serves 10.

Adobong Manok sa Gata

Although many dishes in our neighbor countries of Malaysia and Indonesia are cooked with coconut milk and spiced with hot pepper, this chicken adobo is seasoned just right for us. The degree of spiciness is something that is patently Filipino.

1 1/2 kilo chicken (cut into 12 serving pieces)
1/2 tsp. salt
1/4 tsp. peppercorn
1/2 head garlic, minced
1/2 cup vinegar

2 tbsp. cooking oil
2 cups thick coconut milk
2 - 4 pcs. Jalapena pepper (optional)
Patis (fish sauce) to taste

Marinate chicken in salt, peppercorn, garlic and vinegar overnight. Heat oil and stir-fry chicken. (It is important to stir-fry the chicken first before adding the marinade to improve the flavor.) Next add the marinade, the coconut milk and simmer until sauce thickens. Season with *patis.*

Batangas Adobo

I am including this recipe because, apart from being proud to be a Batangueña, I consider adobo as our national dish. This particular version of the adobo (with achuete or annatto seeds), I am afraid, will soon fade away because it has not been tried as often in the past years. When it does, then a significant part of my childhood will have also faded away.

1/2 kilo beef
200 grams beef heart
100 grams beef liver
1/2 kilo pork
1/2 to 1 cup vinegar, depending on acidity
1 small head garlic
1 tsp. salt
1/2 tsp. black pepper
3 tbsp. *achuete* soaked in 1 cup warm water.

Cut all meats in to serving pieces. In a saucepan, combine vinegar, garlic, pepper, salt. Put in beef and the beef heart. Let cook for 20 minutes. Add pork, beef liver, and *achuete* water and simmer until tender. Strain sauce. Brown the garlic and then the meats in hot oil. Return to saucepan. Cover and simmer until sauce thickens.

Bistek Filipino

I was introduced to **Bistek Filipino** *by a cousin of my father, Carmen Villanueva de Garcia.* She lived near St. Scholastica's College where I was sent to school at the age of three. As I grew older, I would get lunches from Lola Mameng. I would watch her tenderize the beef by beating with the blunt side of her kitchen knife. Then she would blend* calamansi *juice and soy sauce. This has remained a favorite of mine. In Paris, at the Aux Iles Philippines, we served plump tenderloin steaks with this sauce and called the dish* Steak Philippin.

Slices of beef liver can be used marinated in the same mixture of calamansi *juice and soy sauce and pan fried but without overcooking. Overcooking the steak or the liver results in tougher meat and a dried one.*

Calamansi is distinctly Filipino and the mixture of calamansi *and soy sauce is one of our most delicious sauces. We use this unique mixture as marinade (like in the* chicken relleno*) or merely as dipping sauce for fried fish or as flavoring for our* pancit.

(She was the sister of Rafael Villanueva, Batangas representative to the Philippine Congress. They were half-Spanish (mestizo) which is why Uncle Rafael, to emphasize that he was Filipino, always wore the barong Tagalog to Congress instead of the usual coat and tie of that era. Thus he was called "Mr. Barong Tagalog".)*

1/2 k. sirloin, cut into thin slices (against the grain)
3 tbsp. *calamansi* **juice**
1/2 cup soy sauce*

* Soy sauce can have varying degrees of salinity. So, to be sure that the blend is balanced, I mix the soy sauce and *calamansi* in a separate container before I add this to the raw meat.

Prepare the marinade of soy sauce and *calamansi* juice. Correct seasoning. Add this to the sliced beef. Cover and store in the refrigerator for an hour or so. (Marinating overnight may be done, but it is not recommended because sliced beef kept for a long period will have all its juices ooze out).

In a hot pan, fry the beef. Serving beef underdone gives juicier more tender meat. When all the slices have been cooked, add the marinade.

Slices of onions may be fried and added as garnish. The amount of marinade may be doubled and the sauce cooked with onions. Both methods, adding the onions or cooking the onions first, give good results.

Liver in soy: (a variation)
1/2 k. ox liver, sliced
1/2 cup soy sauce
1 - 2 tbsp. *calamansi* **juice (or lemon juice)**
6 slices bacon *
2 large onions sliced into rings

Marinate liver in soy sauce and *calamansi* or lemon juice. Pan fry bacon and set aside. In the bacon fat, saute onion; set aside. Cook liver in remaining hot fat (about 2 -3 minutes) per side. When done, add the marinade and garnish with bacon and onion rings.

* Bacon is optional. It makes this dish Americanized.

Humba (Hong Ba)

Humba *is part of our culinary heritage though it surely originated from the Chinese because of the black beans and peanuts that go into the dish as well as the name which includes the syllable "ba" and which means pork in Chinese. We have translated the recipe to please* our Filipino *palate by covering the bottom of the clay pots in which the* humba *is cooked with banana leaves. Filipinos love to wrap, steam and broil food in banana leaves, and the* humba *is no exception.*

In Leyte, the humba *is cooked in either clay pots or heavy* calderos. *At the bottom of the cooking pot is placed an inverted porcelain plate so that the pork does not stick there when cooked. The dish is popular not only because of its delicious flavor or the way the pork fat almost melts with the long slow cooking but because it keeps for days, an important factor in the era before electricity and refrigeration reached this island province. Like the* adobo, *the* humba *is better tasting days after it is cooked. MF*

1 kilo pork *pigue* or pork *kasim*, whole
2 cloves garlic, minced
1 cup water
2 tbsp. soy sauce
2 tbsp. brown sugar
1 tsp. salt
1/2 cup vinegar
1 sprig oregano
1/2 bay leaf (*laurel*)
1 heaping tbsp. *tausi* (salted black beans)
2 tbsp. fat

Mix all ingredients and cook until pork is tender. Slice pork into serving pieces. Arrange on a platter, set aside. Strain sauce and pour over pork. Serve hot.

Dinuguan

While **dinuguan** *has always been a part of main meals, the trend today is to serve it with* puto* *as a merienda item. The recipe I am sharing with you is from Aling Zeny Balaoro who has a good palate for Filipino blends.*

A good dinuguan *should have pork that is tender, a vinegar flavor that is not pronounced and a smooth sauce that has been carefully cooked so the blood added does not curdle. The traditional way is to add internal organs of the pork. To cut out the difficult part of cleaning intestines, etc. a revised pork recipe is given here where a pig's head may be used. However, any pork cut will do.*

---

2 tbsp. cooking oil
3 cloves garlic, minced
1 onion, minced
1/2 k. pork head, boiled until soft then diced
1 pc. pork heart, boiled then diced
100 gms. pork liver, diced
1/2 - 3/4 cup native vinegar
2 cups broth
1 1/4 cups pork blood
1 cup beef blood
4 pcs. long green *sili* (hot pepper)
1 tbsp. salt
1/2 tsp. msg

Saute garlic in cooking oil add onion, pork head, heart and liver. Pour in vinegar and boil uncovered, without stirring until vinegar has evaporated. Add broth, cover and simmer for 15 minutes. Strain pork and beef blood stirring continuously until thick. Drop *sili*. Simmer 5 minutes more. Season with salt and msg.

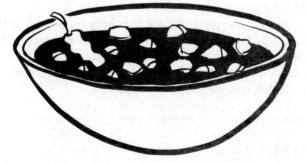

Dinuguan 2: (a variation)

1/2 k. pork
3 cups water with 1/2 tsp. salt
1/2 cup pig's blood
1/2 cup cow's blood
4 tbsp. cooking oil
1 tbsp. pounded garlic
1/2 cup onions, sliced fine
1/2 cup tomatoes chopped
1 radish finely released
1 cup vinegar
salt and pepper to taste

Boil the pork until soft and tender. Reserve 2 cups of the broth. Cut pork into small cubes. Combine the broth, pig's blood and cow's blood. Set aside.

Saute the garlic until golden brown. Then add the onions and tomatoes. Cook for about 10 minutes. Add the boiled pork, radish and vinegar. Cook for 5 - 6 minutes without stirring then add the mixture of blood broth. Season with salt and pepper and stir continuously to prevent the curdling of the blood. Cook for 10 minutes. Serve hot or cold.

Callos

Callos *or tripe is a dish that is similar to the* Tripe a la Mode de Caen, *a classic dish in France. Our* callos, *however, is typically Filipino with the spices and sauces the way we like it.*

A French lady who was also a good cook was very impressed with my version of our Callos. *She hounded me until I gave her the recipe and asked me to cook the dish with her until she learned it.*

Because Callos *takes a lot of time and work to prepare, the dish is served only when one has a feast or has company.*

1 kilo *goto* (tripe)
1 pc. *mukba ng baka* (cow's head)
1 pc. *pata de baka* (ox leg)
salt and vinegar
enough water to cover
2 stalks leeks
6-8 tomatoes
2 medium onions, quartered
4 pcs. carrots, quartered
1/2 cup white wine
1 1/2 tsp. peppercorns
1 1/2 tsp. pimenton powder
1/4 cup olive oil
2 pcs. *chorizo de bilbao* or Spanish sausage, sliced
200 grams bacon, in 1-inch strips
1 pc. *morcillas* or blood sausage, optional
1/4 cup olive oil
4 onions, sliced
2 green pepper, broiled and sliced
2 red pepper, broiled and sliced or *pimientos morrones*, sliced
3/4 cup tomato sauce
Salt to taste
Asparagus tips and red pepper strips (garnishing)

Clean meats with salt and vinegar. Put meats in a large saucepan and add enough water to cover leeks, tomatoes, onions, carrots, white wine, peppercorns and *pimientos*. Cover, let boil over low flame. Simmer until meats are tender.

Heat olive oil. Drop *chorizo de bilbao* and bacon and fry for 5 minutes. Put in *morcillas*, cook 2 minutes more. Set aside.

Saute onions in hot olive oil. Drop in sliced peppers. Add tomato sauce and salt. Simmer 5 minutes and strain. Set aside. When meats are tender, debone and cut up into squares. Put all ingredients together in saucepan, simmer 20 minutes more. Pour into deep serving plate, garnish with asparagus tips and red pepper strips.

Crispy Pata

Probably popularized by the owners of Barrio Fiesta *restaurants, this Filipino favorite has its counterpart in Paris at the world famous* "Pied de Cochon."

One reason for the creation of this dish could be the penchant of the Filipino for the crisp skin of the lechon. *Preparing the* **Crispy Pata** *is similar to that of* Lechon Kawali. *The sauce or* sawsawan *used for this may be a blend of vinegar, soy sauce,* patis, *chili peppers and garlic.*

2 pcs. pork *pata* (front trotters are preferrable because they
    contain more meat)
3 tbsp. coarse salt
1 tsp. msg (optional)
1 tbsp. native vinegar
2 pcs. bay leaf (*laurel*), crushed
1 tsp. black peppercorn, pounded
5 - 6 cups water
2 onions, chopped
Cooking oil for deep-fat frying

Clean pig's feet thoroughly. Make longtitudinal slits on the legs and marinate this in salt, msg, vinegar, bayleaf and pounded black pepper. Keep in the refrigerator for at least 3 hours, turning once in a while to make sure marinade penetrates the meat. Maximum marinating would be 12 hours.

Pour pork feet and marinade into a large pan and add enough water just enough to cover the meat and not too much as to remove all flavors of the meat. Add salt and chopped onions to the water. Let boil then simmer until meat is tender.

Remove *pata* from the pan and hang in cool place to dry or dry under the sun. This will take about 3 to 4 hours.

Once the *pata* has dried, pour oil in a *kawali* and add pork feet and start the heat to cook the *pata*. Cover the *kawali*. The oil will sputter but once this has stopped, remove the cover and continue cooking the other side of the *pata* until it is golden brown and the skin is crisp. Turn *pata* on the other side and repeat procedure. Blisters should have formed on the skin of the *pata*. If not, repeat the process.

Remove from fire when *pata* is crisp. Serve with a sauce made of *patis, toyo*, vinegar and *sili*.

Delicious hamburger

One of my favorite places to have lunch on Sunday (or any day for that matter) was the Taza de Oro *in the days when Miss Hendrick (I have forgotten her first name) was running the place. It was the restaurant which had the best hamburger in town. One day I bought the sandwich and tested and composed a recipe which I felt approximated the hamburger served at this very American restaurant with the Spanish name. Other favorites there included their delicious apple pie (with crust made with Crisco) sometimes served ala mode (with vanilla ice cream) and their* Chili con Carne.

Ditas Lichauco, granddaughter of Doña Luisa Lichauco, complimented me on this recipe saying that it is one of the tastiest hamburger recipes she knows, hence the addition of the adjective "delicious" to the dish.

1/2 k. beef, ground round
1 raw egg
1/2 tsp. mustard
1 - 2 tbsp. Worcestershire sauce
1/4 tsp. salt
1/4 tsp. pepper
1 slice loaf bread
1/4 cup evaporated milk

Tear bread into pieces and soak in milk. Add pepper, salt, worcestershire sauce, egg and mustard. Add mixture to ground beef and knead. Mix well. Pat according to desired shape. Pan fry in a mixture of hot oil and butter. Serve hot.

Morcon

While working on *my first cookbook in 1965, I realized how our cooking has combined well Asian and European cooking. This was when I saw how two condiments blended so naturally in our Philippine cuisine. The* **Morcon,** *in particular, combined well the tomato sauce, which I thought was very Spanish and Italian, with the soy sauce, which at that time was not easily available outside of Asia.*

I shall always remember the Morcon *as the dish my aunt Emilia Villanueva Lapus served to her American friends. It pleased her that they loved her cooking and found* Morcon *specially good. So when I was asked to set up* Maharlika, *the showcase restaurant at the Philippine Center on 5th Avenue in New York City,* Morcon *was one of the steady favorites from the beginning.*

1 kilo beef, sliced as for *morcon* 3/4 inch thick in one piece
2 tbsps. *calamansi* juice
1/4 cup soy sauce
4 pcs. vienna sausage, each cut into 4 diagonally
2 pcs. sweet gherkins or 4 pcs. sweet pickles, cut in thin long strips
2 hard boiled eggs, sliced
100 gms. cheddar cheese, cut in strips
1/2 pc. carrot, cut into long strips
3 slices bacon
2 tbsp. flour
1/4 cup cooking oil
3 bouillon cubes dissolved in 3 cups boiling water
1/4 tsp. salt
1/2 cup tomato sauce

Marinate beef in *calamansi* juice and soy sauce. Arrange strips of vienna sausage, sweet gherkins, hard boiled eggs, cheese, carrots and bacon on marinated beef. Roll neatly and tie with a string. Dredge in flour then brown in hot cooking oil. Transfer to a big saucepan. Add bouillon water. Season with salt. Cover and simmer until beef is tender. Slice, arrange in platter. Pour sauce on top. Garnish with sprigs of parsley. Serve 10.

Calderetta

This is a dish of Spanish origin and the name comes from the Spanish word caldero *which means cooking pot.* **Calderetta** *is often found in fiestas from Batanes to Jolo.*

At the Philippine restaurant I had in Paris, this was one of the popular items which was prepared with lamb shoulder, green olives, liver and other spices.

Our own calderetta *has liver with a touch of chili for added spice. Marinating the meat is an essential step in the preparation of this dish.*

Whether one's favorite is calderetta *made of beef, lamb or goat's meat, the prime objective is to find the blend of flavors that suits one's taste best. Here is a guide to the method generally used for an easy but tasty* calderetta.

1/2 k. *pierna corta* (beef round), cut in serving pieces
1/4 cup vinegar
10 pcs. peppercorn, crushed
1 tsp. salt
2 cloves garlic
1/4 cup cooking oil
1 cup onion, sliced
1/2 cup tomato sauce
1 1/2 - 2 cups boiling water
1 cup red or green pepper, cut into strips
1 pc. *laurel* or bay leaf
dash of hot sauce
1/4 cup liver spread

Marinate beef in mixture of vinegar, peppercorn, salt and crushed garlic for 1 1/2 to 2 hours. Fry pieces of beef in cooking oil. Add onions and saute until tender. Pour in tomato sauce and boiling water. Add the green pepper, bay leaf and hot sauce as desired. Cover and simmer until meat is tender. Blend in liver spread. Cook 5 minutes more. Serves 5.

Kare-kare

In 1965 when I published my first cookbook, I was made aware of what went into the cuisine which we call Filipino. I felt then that the most Filipino of our popular dishes would be **kare-kare**. That was probably because I had traveled mostly to Europe and the United States and found no dish similar to it. Today, as I am learning more about our Asian neighbors, I realized that our kare-kare may have been influenced by the Gado-gado in Indonesia (which has a sauce with peanuts mixed into it) or from an Indian dish called Kadhi.

A friend from India told me that their Kadhi is what the British called Curry and the mixture of spices that go into the dish was mistakenly called as curry powder. She explained how the dish probably was recreated in England from memories of tasty meals in India and that Kadhi was given the name Curry.

Kare-kare has been a favorite since the 1920s and probably even before that. The cooking methods employed and the ingredients of various vegetables, the achuete (annatto seeds),the bagoong and toasted rice are all part of the Filipino's culinary experience.

---

1 ox tail
1 ox leg
6 cups water
1 big onion, quartered
1 stalk celery with leaves, cut up
salt and peppercorns
1/2 cup *achuete* seeds for coloring (annatto seeds)
1/2 cup water
4 pcs. eggplants
1 big bundle *sitao* (string beans)
1 banana heart
1 head garlic, chopped
2 onions, sliced
1/4 cup cooking oil
1/2 cup *bagoong alamang* (salted fermented small shrimps)
1 cup ground peanuts
1 cup toasted ground rice
salt and msg to taste

Boil ox tail and leg in 6 cups water with onions, celery, salt and peppercorns until tender. Cut into desired pieces and set aside. Soak *achuete* seeds in water (1/2 cup); rub to bring out color. Set aside.

Cut vegetables into desired pieces. Boil enough water and drop string beans and parboil. Do likewise with eggplants and banana heart.

Saute garlic and onions in cooking oil. Add *bagoong* and *achuete* water. Let boil 5 minutes. Blend in ground peanuts and ground rice. Bring to boil then put in the meats. Dust before removing from the fire, add the vegetables. Serve with *bagoong guisado*.

Bagoong Guisado:

   1/4 cup cooking oil
   1 head garlic, chopped
   1 onion, chopped
   1/4 kilo boiled pork, diced
   1 1/2 cup bagoong alamang
   1 tsp. sugar
   1/4 cup native vinegar
   14 cup broth from ox tail and leg

Saute garlic and onion in cooking oil. Add the pork, *bagoong* and sugar. Blend well, then add vinegar and broth. Boil until quite dry. Serve with **Kare-kare.**

Bagoong

Every province and every town has its specialties. In Lingayen, it is the *bagoong*.

Vats of fermenting *dilis* occupy one part of the Doria compound. The vats have to stay open or else too many worms may develop. You notice that, even if the vats are open and the smell permeates the air all around, not a single fly is in the place.

The process called *inasinan* is simple—salting *dilis* and then leaving them in vats to ferment.

But it isn't as easy as it seems. The Dorias, however, seem to have the right touch for it and have made their *bagoong* a byword among buyers from Manila, who take liters of both their quality brand *bagoong isda* and the *patis*, and with their neighbors who come to buy as little as 50 centavos worth to give boiled vegetables and grilled fish just the right *bagoong* flavor. Yet their biggest problem is that the *dilis* has become scarce in Pangasinan and have to be imported from other regions. **MF**

Lengua Estofada

*My grandparents (Jose Villanueva y Romualdez and Crescenciana de los Reyes y Chavez) always served **Lengua Estofada** in their Batangas home whenever they had company. A visit from cousins and friends was also an occasion for my lolo to bring out his reserve of wines plus his collection of fruit wines he made himself.*

Estofado reminds me of the French word ettufer which means "to smother." Over the years, estofada has come to mean for me braising in a tightly covered pan, stewing the meat slowly in its juices. In the Philippines, we have added fried potatoes and fried bananas to the estofado. The Lengua *of my childhood in contrast had only slices of mushrooms, very little sauce and with absolutely delicious, tender slices of ox tongue* (lengua). *Each morsel was impregnated with flavor. My grandmother and two aunts were the experts at cooking this dish. I remember the slow cooking over a wood stove in a clay pot fitted with a tight lid.*

Here is my version of our family recipe.

1 ox tongue (1.5 to 2 kilos)
rock salt or cornstarch
1/2 cup soy sauce
1/4 cup vinegar
2 tbsp. brown sugar
1 big onion, sliced
6 pcs. peppercorn, crushed
3 cloves garlic, minced
oil for frying
2 pcs. sliced *chorizo de bilbao*
1/2 cup tomato sauce
1/2 cup olives (optional)
4 pcs. *saba* bananas, quartered and fried

Rub ox tongue with rock salt or cornstarch to remove slime. Rinse in running water. Blanch for 5 minutes in boiling water. Peel or scrape off waxy coating of tongue with a knife. Rinse thoroughly in water.

Marinate tongue in mixture of soy sauce, vinegar, garlic, onions, peppercorns and brown sugar for 1 to 2 hours.

Remove from marinade and fry tongue until golden. Pour off excess oil, leaving 3 to 4 tablespoons in pan. Put back fried tongue in pan. Pour marinade and add enough water to cover. Simmer gently until almost tender, 1 to 1 1/2 hours. Add tomato sauce and olives. Cook another 15 minutes.

To serve, slice tongue and arrange nicely in a platter. Pour sauce over and garnish with fried bananas.

Paella

When I published my cookbook in 1965, **paella** was commonly known as Arroz a la Valenciana. In Spain where this dish originates, the paella is generally a stew of chicken, Seafoods, rice and vegetables flavored with saffron. In Manila where there are many variations of this dish, all the above ingredients, except for the saffron, is included. Glutinous (malagkit), instead of plain rice is also used.

20-25 pcs. clams
2 pcs. crabs (*alimasag*)
300 gms. medium sized shrimps
1 chicken (about 500 gms.), cut up
1/8 cup olive oil
1/4 kilo pork, cut in serving pieces
150 gms. ham, cut in 1 inch squares
1 pc. *chorizo de bilbao*, sliced
4 cloves garlic, crushed
1 medium onion, chopped fine
1 cup tomato sauce
1 1/2 cups rice, washed
3 1/2 cups broth
1 pc. red pepper, in strips
10 pcs. string beans
2 tsp. salt
1 tsp. msg
1/2 cup peas
2 hard boiled eggs
1 sprig parsley
slices of lemon

Boil clams, set aside 1 cup broth.
Boil crabs and shrimps together. Set aside.
Boil bony parts of the chicken. Set broth aside.
Heat olive oil in a steel or a heavy pan or *paellera*. Fry chicken,
pork, ham, and *chorizo*. Cover until half done. Push to one side. Saute
garlic, onion and tomato sauce. Add the broths of clams and chicken
and rice. Mix everything together.

When rice is halfway done, drop the red pepper, string beans, clams.
Season with salt and msg. Cover tightly and allow to cook without
stirring for 20 minutes or until all the broth is absorbed by the rice.
Paella may be baked in the oven. (Keep pan covered).

During the last 5 minutes of cooking, put shrimps, crabs and peas on
top. Garnish with sliced egg, strips of pepper and parsley and lemon
slices.

Native Paella

Bringhe is the Bulacan version of *Arroz
Valenciana* or the *Paella*. *Bringhe* is made of
malagkit rice cooked in coconut milk and then
colored with the rest of the meat and seafood,
not by saffron, as the Spanish do it, but by the
juice of *dilaw* (yellow ginger or turmeric). It
comes out slightly greenish yellow. All ingredients usually found in the *paella* are then mixed
in the *carajay* (*kawali* or wok).

In Cavite, the *Valenciana* is a dish commonly
found during fiestas. It is not mixed with seafood as one would expect of this coastal province. Instead, pork and chicken are added to the
rice and the red coloring is not from tomato
sauce but from the *achuete.*

Other variations may be found in other
provinces. All of them, however, are given a
decidedly Filipino flavoring such as adding *patis*
the way one restaurant in Metro Manila, where
Paella is listed as its specialty, does it. **MF**

Pastel de lengua

Pastel de lengua *is a favorite for dinner parties. The dish used to be served only on special occasions perhaps because of the many steps involved in making it or because not many people then were familiar with the preparation of the pastry that topped the* lengua. *Today, almost all cooks and many homemakers know how to prepare the* Pastel.

There are those who prefer the lengua *with a creamy sauce and those who make it with a brown sauce. Whichever recipe is followed, it is indispensible to have the* lengua *tender. This is one factor that can help assure success with the recipe.*

To cook tongue:
Blanch tongue in boiling water for 10 to 15 minutes. Peel off skin. Allow to simmer slowly in enough water with 1 big sliced onion, salt and msg to taste, 10 pcs. peppercorns and 1 bay leaf, for 3-4 hours or until tender.

Pastry:
2 1/2 cups sifted all-purpose flour
3/4 cup plus 1 tbsp. butter
6 - 8 tbsp. thick cream

Filling:
1/4 cup olive oil
1 big onion, diced
2 med. carrots, pared and cubed
4 med. potatoes, pared and cubed
1/2 cup button mushrooms
1 1/2 - 2 k. cooked ox tongue, cubed
2 pcs. *chorizo de bilbao,* sliced diagonally
2 cups tongue broth
2 tbsp. all-purpose flour
1/2 cup grated cheese
3 tbsp. sherry
1/2 cup green olives
6 pcs. vienna sausage, sliced diagonally

For brushing pastry:
1 eggyolk, slightly beaten
1 tbsp. water

Place flour in a bowl. Cut in the butter until particles resemble coarse meal. Add cream a tablespoon at a time and only enough for particles to stick together and form a ball. Set aside in the refrigerator.

Heat oil in a pan and saute onion until soft; add carrots, potatoes, mushrooms, *chorizos* and cooked tongue. Pour broth, bring to boil and add flour dispersed in a small amount of the broth. Continue cooking until vegetables are cooked.

Stir in sherry, olives and sausage. Cook a little longer. Transfer mixture into a big rectangular pyrex dish. Set aside.

Take pastry dough from refrigerator and roll out into a rectangle between two sheets of waxed paper to approximately one inch bigger than the pyrex dish. Use to cover dish, tucking in edges underneath to fit snugly into the dish then flute.

Brush top of crust with mixture of yolk and water. Make slits to allow steam to escape and bake in a preheated oven 400°F for 20 minutes or until crust turns golden brown.

Pinatisang Manok

Don Alfonso Calalang, former governor of the Central Bank of the Philippines, was an acknowledged connoisseur of good food. Over lunch one day, he was reminiscing about the tasty, fat chicken meat of a bygone era. As usual, I wanted to know about his favorite dish. It is very simple, but he warned me that everything used should be of top quality. To meet Don Alfonso's standards, one must select young, fat native chicken and use the best patis available.

Mention of Don Alfonso Calalang brings to mind one of the most embarasssing moments of my life. When he was governor of Central Bank, we would meet at some social gathering or at a lunch prepared for the gourmets of Manila. At one such luncheon, Don Alfonso pointed to me as the next hostess of the gourmet group. This was to take place about a month and a half later.

In those days, I led a very hectic life doing a daily TV show among other things. At about 10:30 one morning, I noticed that the date was one I had marked with a red letter. It turned out to be the day I was to host the gourmet group meeting. I hurriedly called the secretary of Don Alfonso to ask what time the group was coming that evening. To my dismay, I learned that they were coming to lunch. And I had NOTHING ready!

This must have happened before 1965 when I still had not opened my first French restaurant, Au Bon Vivant, because I had to dash from one restaurant to another. I ordered the first course in one place, dashed to order the main course elsewhere, picked up the dessert somewhere else, then rushed backe to collect my orders. I barely made it to my home and just had enough time to unwrap my orders onto platters.

Don Alfonso, the gentleman that he was, never showed a sign that anything was amiss. I was tortured by the thought that he and the group must have recognized the flavor of the food I served since they were bought from reputable restaurants of the time.

---

1 chicken
2 tbsp. pork lard
Ginger root, cut into strips, about a teaspoon
1/3 cup *patis*
A handful of *sili* leaves
2-3 cups chicken stock

Cut chicken into serving pieces.

In a heavy saucepan (with cover), heat pork fat. Saute ginger strips and add chicken pieces. Brown chicken pieces lightly and add *patis*. Cover pan tightly and lower flame. Allow *patis* to be absorbed. Add chicken stock. Watch carefully to prevent the chicken from drying. There should be enough liquid to make about a cup. When chicken is tender, add *sili* leaves and continue cooking for three (3) minutes more. Serve hot.

Patis

As we become more acquainted with the foods of Southeast Asia, we find so many similarities. And among these would be *patis*, fish sauce that is called *Nyok Mam* in Vietnam and *Nam Pla* in Thailand.

When I opened my restaurant in Paris in 1972, I had to import *patis* as well as *toyo* and *bagoong* from Manila. Today, everything but everything is available in Paris—from *lumpia* wrappers to oyster sauce, fresh fruits (*langka*, durian, lychees) and roasted chestnuts.

What to me is surprising is that in many homes of the younger generation Chinese-Filipinos, *patis* is not found. Instead, light soy sauce is used which is lighter not only in color but also in flavor than the *toyo* (called dark soy sauce) that we are accustomed to.

Food writer Doreen Gamboa Fernandez was most helpful in answering my questions about *patis*. She mentioned that the Japanese anthropologist Namomichi Ishige had made a study on *patis*. Doreen's mother also has been making patis and bagoong for years. In answer to my query on how patis began, Doreen said that it must have been when salt was discovered.

Which then brought me to think about salt

and how it was as precious as gems and spices four centuries ago.

The province of Pangasinan must have been named after the salt beds that abound there and which produce one of the finest and cleanest salts in the country.

And I must include here that the Picasso Museum in Paris is a stunning edifice built from taxes levied on salt and so is nicknamed *Hotel Sale*.

Menudo

Menudo can be prepared with garbanzos*(chickpeas), with* guisantes *(green peas) or simply with potatoes. Recently, I tried* menudo *with* camote *(sweet potatoes) and found it to be seasoned just right for the Filipino taste; a bit on the sweet side because of the* camote. *Even with the kind of meat used,* menudo *has many versions. I have tried using ground beef and ground pork. The most popular version, however, is one that is made with pork, a little pork liver, potatoes,* garbanzos *and tomato sauce.*

The following recipe uses almost all possible ingredients, including green olives and raisins. This is to allow different versions by either reducing or modifying ingredients to suit one's taste, time and budget.

---

800 gms. pork, cut into about 2 cm. cubes
200 gms. pork liver, cut into cubes
3 tbsp. cooking oil
3 cloves garlic
1 - 2 onions, chopped (about 1/2 cup)
1/2 cup tomato paste or 1 cup tomato sauce
1/4 cup vinegar
2 tbsp. soy sauce
2 - 4 tbsp. brown sugar
2 cups pork or chicken stock or water

1/2 tsp. salt
1/2 tsp. pepper
2 bay leaves
1 big red bell pepper, cut in strips
3 - 4 pcs. potatoes, diced (about 300 gms.)
1 cup chick peas (*garbanzos*), cooked and peeled
10 pcs. green olives (optional)
1/2 cup raisins

Heat cooking oil. Saute the garlic and onions. Add tomato paste, vinegar, soy sauce, brown sugar and pork or chicken stock. Add the pork but set aside the liver. When pork is tender, season with salt, pepper and bay leaves. Mix the rest of the ingredients including the liver.

Puchero, Cocido

In my research on Spanish dishes incorporated into our menu, I have come across several, among them the Cocido, Paella, Pochero, *and the* Calderetta.

The **Cocido** *and* **Pochero** *are quite similar and some have confused one with the other. I have asked various Spanish friends to help me differentiate the two. Some of them have told me that* Cocido *is a stew of beef while* Pochero *uses chicken.*

I have made my own distinction between the two.

Pochero *is our stew of pork, chicken and beef, flavored with* chorizo *and served with* camote *and eggplant sauce.*

Cocido *is also a stew of beef, pork, chicken and sausages but added to it is ham,* garbanzos, *cabbage and carrots. It is served with* Tomatada *a rich, slowly stewed tomato sauce with a hint of olive oil.*

Cocido, *by the way, is prepared in different fashions in the various regions of Spain. The words* cocido, olla *and* escuella *all mean stew in Spanish.*

Cocido

1/2 kilo beef shank *(bias)*
1 kilo soup bones
1 chicken (about 1 kilo)
1/2 kilo lean pork *(pigue)*
1 tsp. peppercorn
3 pcs. tomatoes, quartered
3 stalks leeks (about 200 gms.)
3 onions, quartered
1 head garlic, crushed
3 tbsp. olive oil
200 gms. bacon, cut in chunks
3 pcs. *chorizo de bilbao*
1 *morcilla* or Spanish blood sausage
1/2 kilo potatoes
1/2 kilo cabbage
1/2 kilo Baguio pechay or Chinese cabbage
2 pcs. carrots
1/4 kilo string beans

Boil beef and soup bones with 1 stalk leek, 1 tsp. peppercorn, tomato and onion. When beef is tender, remove and cut into serving pieces. Set broth aside.

Boil chicken and pork separately with the same ingredients. Prepare Spanish tomato sauce.

Combine beef, chicken and pork broth. Let boil. Add softened meats, *chorizo de bilbao* and *morcillas*. Simmer. In another pan, cook vegetables until half done in beef and chicken broth. Add to meats and cook until done.

Arrange meat and vegetables on a platter. Serve with broth and Spanish tomato sauce.

Spanish Tomato Sauce:
1/4 cup olive oil
3 cloves garlic, crushed
4 large onions, chopped
1 cup tomatoes, chopped
1 cup tomato sauce
1 cup broth
salt and pepper
msg

Saute garlic, onions and tomatoes in olive oil. Cook till tender. Add tomato sauce and simmer for 10 minutes. Add broth and seasonings. Cook slowly for 1 hour in a covered container.

Puchero Filipino
with Eggplant sauce

1/2 kilo pork round or belly, cut into serving pieces
1/2 kilo chicken, cut into serving pieces
1/2 kilo beef shank, cut into serving pieces
2 pcs. *chorizo de bilbao*
5 cups water
1 tsp. salt
1 small bunch green onions
2 tbsp. cooking oil
4 cloves garlic
1 medium onizon, sliced
salt and pepper to taste
4 cups broth (from cooking meats)
1 small cabbage
1/4 kilo green beans
4 small boiled potatoes, pared and halved
4 pcs. boiled *saba* bananas, peeled and quartered
1 cup canned or boiled *garbanzos* (chick peas)

Eggplant sauce:
6 small eggplants, broiled, peeled and mashed
3 cloves garlic, minced
1/4 cup vinegar
salt and pepper to taste

Boil meats in water with salt and green onions until tender. Drain and reserve broth. Set the meats aside.

Heat oil and saute garlic and onions until soft. Add seasonings and broth. Bring to boil and add cabbage and green beans. Cook a few minutes then add meats, boiled potatoes, bananas and *garbanzos*. Adjust seasonings and cook for a few minutes. Dish out meats and vegetables in separate mounds in a platter; serve broth in a tureen. Accompany with eggplant sauce prepared simply by mixing all the ingredients for sauce.

Finadene Sauce

A slim cookbook on the Cuisine of Guam was sent to me by Dorothy Horn. Many of Horn's recipe are Filipino in origin which is not surprising since a large percentage of Guam's population came from the Philippines.

They serve *Bistek* (beef steak) and *Escabeche* fish. Corn pudding is called *calamay*. And their fiesta table consist of *pancit* (pronounced, writes Horn, as *panseai*) and which the author describes as "by way of the Philippines by way of China," fried *lumpia*, pork *adobo* and *empanada*.

Perhaps one noticeable ingredient in many of their recipes is the chili pepper making their dishes akin to our Bicol cuisine. And the chili pepper takes center stage in Guam's unique sauce. Horn says that "there is no other sauce in the world like Guam's own Finadene sauce... This volatile sauce adds spice and flavor to everything. There are innumerial variations and recipes. Here are just two. Take it easy when first using, it tends to sneak up on you and packs a wallup like a mallet to your head. BUT GOOD!!!"

I have reproduced both sauce versions here making some slight corrections from the original because Horn's excitement about the sauce made her forget some of the important procedures.

Finadene Sauce I
10 - 12 medium hot peppers
1/3 cup soy sauce
1/2 cup lemon juice
1/2 cup chopped onions

Mash hot peppers. Either mash a few or all depending on the "hotness" you want to achieve. Add the rest of the ingredients and keep covered in the refrigerator. Serve as is. Yield 1 scant cup.

Finadene Sauce II
10 - 12 chili peppers
1/2 cup chopped onions
2 cloves garlic, mashed
1/2 cup coconut milk

Mash peppers, garlic and onions. Add coconut milk and serve. Onions can be added later or just before srving. (Hang on to your hat because this is one REAL blast.)

ANGELES

MECHADO A LA ANGELES
FOOD FOR THE GODS
PIGEON PIE
ROPA VIEJA
TAYLOR POT ROAST
BREAD PUDDING
INSTANT CORN SOUP
WITH QUAIL EGGS
CHICKEN SPAGHETTI
SEAFOOD BROCHETTE
BEEF AND LENTIL STEW
ENSAYMADA ESPESYAL

S HORTLY BEFORE *my last trip to Paris in December 1990, I visited with my mother-in-law, Doña Angeles Ortega de Daza who was sick in bed. She was then one month shy of being 90 years old. We talked a while and when I asked her about the lessons she had under Doña Luisa Lichauco who she said taught her the basics, she told me that she still had her notes and old cookbooks. I asked her if I could have them. She then directed her nurse to get them and she handed them to me. They are yellowed with age with the binding already loose. But they are now part of my most precious possessions and provide a link with our culinary past which I had been seeking.*

It was Doña Angeles who taught me a lot of the very good recipes included in my first cookbook. She had made it her life's work to prepare and serve her family the best dishes she could. When she married Don Gabriel Daza Sr., she knew just a few native dishes. But she studied and when I met her, she was one of the best cooks I knew. What was more, she shared with me everything she knew. A year after my visit, she died. I was in Paris then and I remember most one remark she made. She said: "My favorite daughter-in-law is my first." That was me!

I treasure the heritage she left me and appreciate the debt I owe her. Much of my knowledge about good food got a tremendous boost from her cooking. This is why I am dedicating this portion of the book to her.

I was told that on the last day of the Novena for her, the Daza family gathered to prepare a dinner featuring the dishes they remembered she used to cook. These included Paella, Relleno, Picadillo, *Lentil soup,* Cannelones, Bacalao, Inihaw na Talong sa Gata, *Leche* Flan *and* Chicken Relleno.

Mechado a la Angeles

This recipe bears the given name of my mother-in-law as a tribute to her. Her life was devoted to shopping for and then cooking the best food for her family.

Should you dare try this recipe without larding your beef with pork fat (mitcha), the slices of the **mechado** *will not look the same and it will not taste the same. I know. When I made the pork fat stew in the sauce, I did not get the same taste nor the same dish.*

---

1 kilo beef round (*kabilugan*) larded with 4-6 strips of pork fat
4 big onions, quartered
3/4 cup tomato sauce
1/2 cup soy sauce
2 cups beef stock or 2 cubes beef bouillon and 2 cups water
1 pc. bay leaf
4 potatoes, quartered and fried
1/4 cup oil

In a deep saucepan, heat oil. Place meat and brown on all sides. Pour out excess oil. Add rest of the ingredients and continue cooking till done. Slice and serve with the sauce.

Food for the Gods

On the cover of the yellowed 1930 Bureau of Education notebook is the beautiful but unmistakably Assumption school writing of my mother-in-law. She had placed her pre-war address in Ermita as #808 Georgia. When I read that, I realized that we were almost next door neighbors because my parents lived in a house at the corner of Vermont, the home they stayed in when I was born.

On the same cover were these words: Cooking lessons under the direction of Doña Luisa Lichauco. The lessons were always given in complete menus. The filled notebooks even had three complete Christmas menus.

Three of the dishes there stand out for me. These were Roast Turkey, **Food for the Gods** *and* Ensaimada. *There are three different recipes for* ensaimada *and four for Roast Turkey.*

I am rewriting here the recipe for Food for the Gods.

Prepare a baking pan 13" by 9" by greasing it and lining with wax paper.

6 egg whites
6 egg yolks
2 cups sugar in portions of 1 3/4 and 1/4
2/3 cups soda crackers, crushed
2 tsp. baking powder
1 1/2 kilos chopped walnuts
1 1/2 cups dates, cut up in tiny pieces
1 tsp. vanilla
whipped cream (optional)

Prepare cracker crumbs by rolling crackers between two layers of wax paper and pressing the broken pieces with a rolling pin. This should give you coarse crumbs. Sift through a sifter with large holes, enough to make the required 2/3 cup. Set aside.

Beat egg yolks until blended and add 1 3/4 cups sugar gradually. The mixture should end up lemon colored. Add the measured cracker crumbs, baking powder, chopped walnuts and cut dates. Blend thoroughly. Set aside.

Beat egg whites till bubbles are even and it has risen to its maximum volume. Add the remaining 1/4 cups sugar. (This helps to stabilize the egg whites). Continue beating until the whites are stiff but not dry. It should remain glossy looking. Add the vanilla. Carefully fold in the yolk mixture of walnuts and dates. Pour into prepared baking pan. It should be 1.2 inch thick and the batter must touch the sides of the container.

(From my mother-in-law's notes she says: "Let the mold fall twice on the board." This means to pound the pan on the table twice so as to let the air pockets escape and assure that the product will be even-grained.)

Bake in an oven at 350°F for over an hour.

* As you will notice, this baked dessert does not have any flour but the cracker crumbs. The idea is to cook the eggs with the heavy mixture of walnuts and dates. This is a much lighter product than a pudding. This dessert has been a part of many family gatherings and so I am including this in my culinary autobiography.

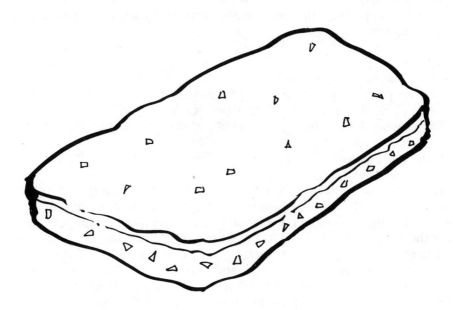

Pigeon Pie

Early in my married life, I was invited by my in-laws to a sit-down dinner at their home. What stands out in my memory was the **Pigeon Pie** *that was served. Here is the recipe.*

Select 8 pigeons (but plan on one pigeon per guest). If you have big but tender pigeons, you may cut them in half.

8 pigeons
16 slices of bacon
25 - 30 potato balls, fried
8 hard-boiled eggs, cut in halves, crosswise
1/4 cup Bovril (a meat concentrate or a demi-glace stock)
1 - 1 1/2 cups pigeon stock, made from the wings and feet of the pigeon

Fry bacon till just crisp. Set aside.
Prepare pigeon by cutting off the bony parts (wings and feet). Boil these to make the stock. Clear and strain stock.
The pigeon is then fried (either whole or in halves depending on the size) in bacon fat. Half-cook only. Set aside.
Make a pie dough to cover the dish. (The two-cup recipe for Pie Crust will do. See page 138).
Prepare an oven-proof dish which is big enough to snuggly fit in the pigeons. Arrange the fried pigeons in the baking dish. Arrange the hard-boiled eggs over the pigeons and scatter the fried potato balls all over the dish. Add the Bovril to the clear and strained pigeon stock. Arrange the bacon strips over each of the pigeons.
Cover the dish with the pie crust and seal the sides. Cut slits on the top of the dish to allow steam to escape while baking. Brush the top with a mixture of egg or milk to give the crust a nice sheen.
Bake in a moderate oven of 350°F until the crust is golden brown. Allow the dish to stand for about 15 minutes so that flavors will settle and the dish will not be too hot but serve while the dish is still hot.

Ropa Vieja

Even my father-in-law, Don Gabriel Daza Sr. nurtured my culinary inclination by lending me a cookbook from the old Philippine Manufacturing Company. Most of the recipes had ingredients that included Purico (lard) and Star margarine. There are recipes for ensaimada, bunnuelos, churros, glorias and pilipit including breads, cakes and dishes most average Americans prepared in the Philippines.

The most interesting portion of this PMC cookbook was called the NEPA recipes. These include Arroz a la Valenicana, Arroz a la Cubana, Kari de Pata, Pollo Asado de Carajay, Batchoy, Pakam, Kilawin in four versions, empanada, chicken tinola, fish cardillo, lumpia, asado. caldereta, paklay, dinuguan, and lengua estofada.

The cookbook recorded the dishes that Filipinos of the time, and even up to now, truly love.

I tried the memorable **Ropa Vieja** *at the house of the late Dean and Mrs. Patrocinio Valenzuela. Mrs. Valenzuela loved to cook and while I may no longer have her original recipe, I know that she said the dish was made of left-over meats, about 2 cups in all. They must have given the name ropa vieja to the dish because the term is Spanish for "old clothes."*

---

2 cups cooked meats
2 tbsp. cooking oil or lard (lard makes a better tasting dish)
4 cloves garlic
1/2 cups chopped onions
1/4 cup chopped tomatoes or 1/4 cup vinegar

Saute garlic till just light brown. Add onions until they become translucent. Stir in the tomatoes or vinegar. Simmer together for about 2 minutes. Add the cooked meats and stir the mixture occasionally.

* The best *Ropa Vieja* is made by cooking the meats slowly so that the dish becomes almost dry. A tasty, different meat dish is then obtained from left-overs. But if you should want to make this dish and have no meat left-overs, try using boiled beef or ground cooked beef.

I have asked my children for their recipes and am including them here. They have taken to cooking at an early age too and I would like to think that my mother-in-law and I did have some influence there. This is also their way of paying tribute to their grandmother whose caring was expressed mainly in her cooking.

Included too is a recipe from Sylvia Cancio Lim, my partner at our restaurant, Mai Thai. The ensaymada espesyal she has contributed is, after all, an original recipe of my mother-in-law's cooking teacher, Doña Luisa Lichauco.

Taylor Pot Roast

Mariles Daza Taylor is a graduate of the University of Florida, major in Restaurant Management. She is presently based in San Francisco and is working with United Airlines. She has a three-year-old boy, Eduardo.

1 1/2 kilo pork *pigue*

Marinade:
   2 cloves garlic, sliced
   1/2 cup soy sauce
   1/4 tsp. pepper

   1/2 tsp salt
   1/2 tsp. pepper
   1/2 cup flour
   1/2 cup cooking oil
   1/2 cup water
   2 tbsp. cornstarch dispersed in
   2 tbsp. water

Tie pork with string to shape like a ham. Bore holes in pork meat and insert slivers of garlic about 1 1/2 inches apart. Marinate with soy sauce and pepper overnight.

Combine salt, pepper and flour. Roll pork into the mixture.

Heat cooking oil. Fry pork until brown then add 1/2 cup water. Seal in tight covered pan and simmer until tender. Add cornstarch dispersed in 2 tbsp. water to thicken sauce. Blend the sauce, slice the meat and serve.

Bread Pudding

Stella Daza Belda is a graduate of the University of the Philippines with a Bachelor of Arts degree. She hosts my TV show, "Cooking it up with Nora." Stella is married to Jay Belda. They have three children, Toby, Bettina and Bolo.

(Don't throw leftover *pandesal.* You may keep them in a plastic bag and refrigerate but make sure these remain dry beause wet *pandesal* may develop mold).

5 cups old *pandesal*, cut in slices (leftover biscuits may be added
1big can condensed milk
1 big can evaporated milk
1/2 cup water
4 whole eggs
1 cup sugar
1 tsp. vanilla
1/2 cup raisins (optional)

Soak sliced *pandesal* and leftover biscuits in condensed and evaporated milk and water for 10 minutes. Then mash with hands. Add remaining ingredients and pour on a 9x9 baking pan lined with:

1/2 cup butter, softened
1/2 cup brown sugar
1 tbsp. cinnamon powder

Combine butter, sugar and cinnamon in a bowl and spread on the bottom of your baking pan. Bake at 350°F for 30 minutes.

Instant Corn Soup
with Quail Eggs

6 cups water
4 pcs. chicken bouillon cubes
1 can cream of corn
1/2 medium-sized carrot, finely chopped
2 dozens, quail eggs, hard-cooked
1 egg, slightly beaten
salt and pepper to taste
3 tbsp. cornstarch dispersed in 3 tbsp. water

Boil water and bouillon cubes. Add cream of corn, grated carrots and quail eggs. Wait for the soup to boil then add the beaten egg while stirring the soup. Season with salt and pepper. Thicken with corn-starch.

Chicken Spaghetti

3 tbsp. cooking oil
1 mediu-sized onion, sliced
1 pc. *chorizo de bilbao*, sliced
4 slices sweet ham, cut in 1/2 " squares
3 eggs, hard cooked, finely chopped
1 whole chicken, cut in half
2 medium-sized onions, quartered
1 tsp. whole peppercorns
1 tbsp. rock salt
9 cups water
1 can (385 gms.) tomato sauce
1/2 cup grated cheese
1 pack (450 gms.) spaghetti noodles

Saute onions, *chorizo de bilbao* and sweet ham in oil. Set aside. Meanwhile boil chicken in 9 cups of water, with quartered onions, rock salt and peppercorns. When chicken is cooked, remove it from the stock and shred the chicken meat. Strain stock to remove pepperorns and onions then boil the chicken stock under medium heat. When the stock starts to boil add 1 pack of uncooked noodles, chopped hard cooked eggs, tomato sauce, and the *chorizo de bilbao*,-sweet ham mixture. Continue cooking until noodles are *al dente*. Add grated cheese. Blend well then remove from fire.

Seafood Brochette

Nina Daza Puyat graduated with a degree in Hotel and Restaurant Management at the Cornell University in Ithaca, New York. She hosts my TV show, "Cooking it Up with Nora" and is co-author of The Philippine Cookbook. *Nina is married to Louie Puyat and they have two children, Gio and Billie.*

1/2 kilo large prawns, shelled
1/2 kilo large squid, peeled and cut into 1 inch rings (save tentacles for anothr dish)
1/'2 kilo *lapu-lapu* fillet, cut into match box size cubes
3/4 cup virgin olive oil
2 tbsp. brandy
1 tsp. Italian seasoning or a few sprigs of fresh dill
1/2 tsp. salt
freshly ground pepper
skewers or barbecue sticks

Marinate prawns, squid and fish in olive oil, brandy and seasonings overnight. Skewer alternately into sticks or metal skewers. Broil over charcoal for 3 - 4 minutes on each side. Serve with lemon wedges. Makes 6 - 8 servings.

Beef and Lentil Stew

1 kilo beef shank or beef spareribs
6 cups water
2 onions, quartered
1/4 cup olive oil
1/2 head garlic, crushed
1 onion, chopped
5 - 6 pcs. *chorizo de bilbao*, sliced diagonally
1 1/2 cups lentils, soaked in 4 cups of water overnight
4 cups beef stock
1/4 cup white wine
1 *laurel* leaf
 1/2 - 3/4 tsp. salt
1/4 tsp. pepper

Put beef and onions in a deep sauce pot. Add water and bring to a
boil. Cover and simmer for about 3 hours or until meat is tender.
Reserve stock.

In another pot, heat oil. Saute garlic until light brown. Add onions
and cook until translucent. Toss in sliced chorizos and then lentils.
Pour in beef stock and put back the softened meat. Add white wine,
laurel, salt and pepper. Cover and simmer for at least 30 minutes more,
stirring constantly.

Makes 6 - 8 servings.

Ensaymada Espesyal

1 tbsp. yeast
2/3 cup lukewarm water
1 tbsp. sugar
1 cup all-purpose flour
1/2 cup fresh milk
1 cup butter
1 cup sugar
12 egg yolks

1 cup grated *queso do bola*
5 cups all-purpose flour
1/4 cup Wesson butter-flamed oil
Additional butter for brushing
Additional sugar and grated cheese

Dissolve 1 tbsp. yeast in 2/3 cup lukewarm water. Add 1 tbsp. sugar. Let stand 10 minutes.

Add in 1 cup all-purpose flour. Mix well. Let rest for 20 minutes.

In the meantime, scald 1/2 cup fresh milk, 1 cup butter, and 1 cup sugar. Cool immediatly. Add in 12 eggyolks after the mixture has cooled.

Add the yeast mixture to the above mxiture. Then add 1 cup grated *queso de bola*. Mix with wooden spoon and slowly add 5 more cups of flour. Lastly, add 1/4 cup *Wesson* butter-flamed oil.

Transfer to mixer, knead with a dough hook at low speed. Add a little more flour if mixutre is too soft.

Form the dough in a ball and mix with a little butter while kneading. Place in a buttered foil. Cover and let rise until dough mixture doubles (about 1 1/2 hours0.

Divide dough into 20 pieces (for medium *ensaymada* molds). Roll each piece out thinoly into a rectangular shape. Mush in butter. Roll into shape and lock the ends under to seal. Place in greased mold (to grease use shortening). Let rise until double in size.

Bake at 323°F for 15 minutes. Cool. Brush with melted butter. Sprinkle with sugar and grated cheese.

Cacao and chocolate

Cacao is part of my childhod memories. My grandmother had several trees surrounding her home. My cousins and I would watch the elongated pods get heavier and bigger. I remember them hanging from the trees and when we could pick them, we would burst them open then suck and squeeze out the whitish succulent seeds clinging to the central membrane. The seeds would be something like mangosteen seeds though slightly less flavorful. After that, we would spit out the seeds and these would be dried under the sun as a first stage to making cocoa tablets. After being sun dried, we would toast the seeds until they were golden brown and then ground them to the consistency of peanut butter. Sugar would be added and the cocoa mixture would be shaped into tablets also called *tablia*.

To this day, there are homes in Batangas City where the family has chocolate tablets available all the time. An impromptu visit there still allows me to enjoy the chocolate of my youth with tiny bits of the toasted cocoa suspended in milk. Little touches like these evoke treasured moments of the days when life was gracious and more leisurely paced.

SALAD

PAMPANGO FROZEN FRUIT SALAD
GREEN MANGO SALAD
SOM TUM (PAPAYA SALAD)
RUSSIAN SALAD
RED EGGS AND TOMATO SALAD
SALSA MONJA
PINEAPPLE BUKO SALAD
SALAD NICOISE
COLESLAW
CAESAR SALAD

S ALADS AND ensaladas *are definite imports from Spain and the United* *States. Whatever native salads we had would include vegetables* *flavored with* calamansi, *salt, or* bagoong. *As in our* sinigang, *the souring ingredient used (to balance the salad dressing) would be any or all of the following: vinegar,* calamansi, camias, *green mango.*

In our Thai restaurant, we use the green mangoes in many salads which are received with hearty acclaim by many of our guests. Since the Nineties seems to find Thai cooking at the center stage of world cuisine, we will include a few salads from Thailand.

Pampanga Frozen Fruit Salad

(The best intro to this recipe was written years ago. It was another introduction I was asked to write, this time for a book, Culinary Arts in the Tropics Circa 1922.*)*

I had a sense of truimph when I saw the recipe for **Frozen Fruit Salad***. My own version in my cookbook,* Let's Cook With Nora *had evoked comments because the recipe included mayonnaise. I rechecked my recipe which was gleaned from my Guanzon relatives in Pampanga. It seems as close to the salads that were served to me as a child. With the* Frozen Fruit Salad *of Circa 1922, I can heave a sigh and smile for I know the version I had was correct and came from an era before mine.*

2 cups fruit cocktail
1 cup Queen Anne cherries (maraschino)
1 cup peaches in 1 inch cubes
1 cup pineapple chunks
1 cup fresh apples, in 1 inch cubes, marinated in juice or syrup to prevent discoloration
1 cup *lacatan* banana sliced, marinated in juice or syrup
1/4 kilo grapes, peeled
orange sections
chopped almonds
1 cup thick cream, whipped stiff
1/2 to 1 cup mayonnaise

Chill all fruits all dipped in syrup or juice to prevent discoloration or drying out. When chilled, drain all fruits. Be careful to keep each piece of fruit intact. Set aside.

Fold in whipped cream into mayonnaise. Carefully fold whipped mixture into fruits. Arrange salad in bowl and garnish with *maraschino* cherries.

Fruit salad may be served as is. Or freeze, then serve. Serves 12.

Green Mango Salad
(Yam Mamuang)

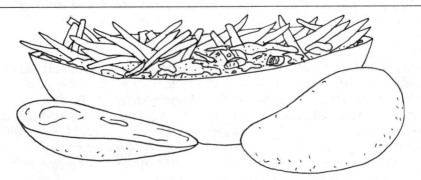

4 green mangoes, peeled, cored and thinly sliced
1/2 lb. *singkamas*, peeled and thinly sliced
1 tsp. salt
juice of 2 limes (*dayap*)
1 tbsp. peanut oil
5 cloves garlic, crushed and thinly sliced
6 green onions (including some of the green), thinly sliced
1/2 lb. ground pork
1 tbsp. shrimp powder*
4 tbsp. *nam pla* (fish sauce or *patis*)
4 tbsp. chunky peanut butter
2 tbsp. palm or brown sugar
1/4 tsp. ground black pepper
1/2 tsp. dried red chili flakes

Put the green mango and *singkamas* slices into a mixing bowl and sprinkle with salt and lime juice.

In a frying pan, heat the peanut oil and fry the garlic and green onions until the garlic is just cooked. Remove with a slotted spoon and set aside to drain. In the same hot oil, fry the ground pork until the pink disappears. Add the powdered shrimp, fish sauce, peanut butter and sugar. Stir well and remove from the heat.

Combine the cooked ingredients from the saucepan to the marinating fruits/tubers in the mixing bowl. Add the pepper and chili flakes. Mix thoroughly. Chill in the refrigerator and serve cold.

* Shrimp powder from *hibe* (dried shrimp) which is pounded and sifted.

Som Tum
(Papaya Salad)

2 medium-size green *papayas*
6 cherry tomatoes
1 clove garlic
1 knob fresh ginger
2 fresh red chilis
2 fresh green chilis
200 gms. roasted chicken meat
crisp lettuce leaves
75 ml. fresh lime juice
25 ml. *nam pla* (fish sauce or patis)
50 gms. palm sugar
25 gms. *hibe*, (dried shrimps) finely chopped
25 gms. roasted peanuts, chopped
sprigs of fresh parsley

Peel the *papaya*. Remove the seeds and cut the flesh into thin slices. Quarter the tomatoes and finely chop the garlic and ginger.

Finely chop 1 red and 1 green chili and cut the remaining two chilis into fine julienne strips.

Arrange the lettuce leaves on a serving plate.

Combine the lime juice, *nam pla* and sugar in a large mixing bowl and stir until the sugar has completely dissolved. Add the garlic, ginger and chopped chili. Stir well, then remove half the dressing and set to one side.

Place the sliced green *papaya* and tomato in a bowl and toss well. Transfer the *papaya* and tomato to the serving plate and sprinkle with the finely chopped *hibe* and roasted penaut. Arrange the pieces of chicken on top and pour on the remaining salad dressing. Garnish with julienne strips of chili. Chill slightly before serving.

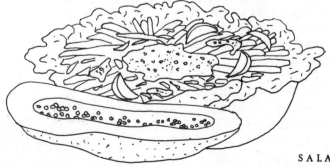

Russian Salad

Coming home from St. Scholatica's College where my sisters and I attended school in the early 1930's, I was surprised to find house guests I had never met. They were an uncle of my father, Rafael Villanueva, and his Spanish wife who caused all the fuss. He had been married to an elegant lady before but they had parted ways. After that he went to Spain where he met his present wife and had come home also with their daughter. They lived with us for a while.

Encarnacion was his wife's name but we called her Encarna. She spoke Spanish at such a fast clip that I remember having had to figure out what she was saying. We did speak Spanish at home but then I never had it thrown at me at machine-gun pace.

Encarna bragged about her cooking so we had dishes with mayonnaise and olive oil galore. What stood out was her Ensalada Russa which she used to say as "Aayy, her forte." Just imagine this Madrilena and her "r"s for "Russa."

After half a century, I now know that her special potato salad was called Russian because of the red beets, a staple in most Russian cuisine such as Borstch.

My recipe of Russian salad in previous cookbooks is titled Royal Russian Salad. I can't tell why I called it Royal.

Russian salad in the French Larousse Gastronimique (the French classic when it comes to cuisine) states that Russian salad is a mixture of vegetables, pickled tongue, sausages, mushrooms, lobster and truffles. Now that deserves the adjective "royal."

For the Filipino version, however, we like it for its simpler ingredients mixed with very good mayonnaise.*

---

2 c. cooked potatoes, cubed
1 c. cooked carrots, diced
1 c. cooked stringbeans, in 1/4" pcs.
1 c. sweet peas, drained
1 c. sweet mixed pickles
1 c. cooked chicken, shredded
1-2 c. mayonnaise*
1 c. cooked beets, diced
1 hard cooked egg, sliced
Few leaves head lettuce
Sprig of parsley

In a bowl, toss lightly first 6 ingredients together. Moisten with mayonnaise. Put in beets and toss with more mayonnaise. Mold salad and serve cold on a bed of crisp lettuce. Garnish with hard cooked egg slices and sprigs of parsley.

To make your own mayonnaise, the best appliance would be a blender. But this can be made using only a bowl and a fork or a wire whip.

Start with two egg yolks. Add prepared mustard and pour salad oil in tiny dribbles. Once I get a small batch beaten and emulsified in my bowl, I can add more oil gradually in larger quantities.

My food guru from my University of the Philippines days, Professor Matilde de la Paz Guzman drummed into me that the amount of oil I could add to my mayonnaise should be just slightly less that the amount in my bowl.

To play safe, I add the oil to my thickened mayonnaise already so that it is incorporated into the emulsion before I add more oil. After I have a thick emulsion, I add my seasonings — vinegar, salt, mustard, white pepper.

Red Eggs and Tomato Salad

8 pcs. big red tomatoes, cut in halves
1 pc. medium radish
1/4 cup *bagoong alamang*, cooked
1 cup sliced tomatoes
3 red eggs, sliced
parsley or *kinchay*

Scoop seeds from tomatoes which have been cut in halves. Set aside. Peel radish. Squeeze with salt then wash with water.

Mix cooked *bagoong* with sliced tomatoes and radish. Put the mixture inside the tomato halves; put the sliced red egg on top. Cover with the other half of the tomato. Decorate with parsley or *kinchay* on top. Serve cold.

Salsa Monja

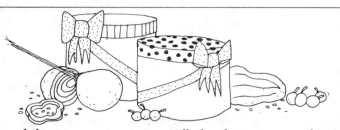

Once in a while, one comes across really lovely persons and I treasure them dearly. Tita Bebeng Roces (Doña Isabel Roces) was one such lady. She was the prima donna of the powerful Manila Times publishing firm before the Marcoses dismantled that venerable institution. And all because an in-law was supposed to have snubbed someone. Miss Roces was the sister of Chino Roces and was known as the "Grand Dame of the Manila Times" a title given to her because many believed that it was she who called the shots at the newspaper.

Very early in my career, I was asked by Ms. Luisa Linsangan, editor of the Women's magazine to join DZWS, a radio station owned by the Manila Times and whose programming was geared to women listeners. I was to do a homemaker's program as well as another which was called "At Home with the Stars." Very often, Tita Bebeng would invite me and the stars who were my guests to join her for lunch. During one of those times, she shared with me one of her favorite recipes, the **salsa monja.**

Someone who shared the same recipe with me was a bosom friend of Tita Bebeng, another unforgettable person, Doña Remedios Ozamis Fortich who was congresswoman of Bukidnon. When Doña Remedios visited Manila I met her often and learned to appreciate her naughty but nice sense of humor. There is a story that shows just how naughty she was.

Whenever Congresswoman Fortich rode her jeep through the rough and sometimes non-existent roads in Bukidnon, she had to wear slacks or pants. At that time, slacks were only worn for outings. When she could not go home to change for Sunday mass, she would rush to church still wearing her rugged attire. The parish priest called her attention to this and her retort was: "Father, would you rather I attended Mass without my pants?" Later, as a compromise, she always brought a skirt along with her and would wear it over her pants.

I had lost the original salsa monja recipe but was able to retrieve it from Tita Bebeng's niece, Nena Roces Verzosa who is now Mrs. Sergio Barrera, wife of a Philippine diplomat. This is the Roces version of the salsa monja.

1 1/2 cups bread crumbs
1 cup olive oil
1 cup juice of sweet mixed pickles or lemon juice
2 tbsp. finely pounded garlic
2 tbsp. salt
1/2 cup green olives
1/2 cup small peeled *sibuyas* Tagalog or shallots
1/2 cup chopped green onions
2 tbsp. paprika
1/2 cup olive oil
1/2 cup juice of sweet mixed pickles
more salt to taste

Sift bread crumbs and place these into a clean jar with a cover. Add the next 8 ingredients (except the additional salt and the last 1/2 cup olive oil and the 1/2 cup juice of sweet mixed pickles.) Shake all the ingredients in a bottle and store in the refrigerator for a day or two. Once the ingredients have blended thoroughly, add the remaining olive oil and pickle juice. Adjust the taste by adding salt and more paprika if needed.

Pimiento may be added for more color and lemon juice can be used.

The *salsa monja* keeps well in the refrigerator. It is delicious with fish.·

Pineapple Buko Salad

1 can condensed milk
2 egg yolks
2 cups *buko* meat (young coconut)
2 cups pineapple tidbits
1 cup *kaong* (sugar palm), boiled until tender
1 can lychee (fruit cut into halves)

Make salad dressing by cooking condensed milk and egg yolks over double boiler until thick. Stir continuously. Cool. Blend *buko*, pineapple, *kaong*, lychee and salad dressing. Pour into pan and chill. Serve cold.

Salad Nicoise

This is a salad that was named after Nice, France. The combination of ingredients is a very happy choice for the flavors blend and contrast perfectly. Nice, found in the south of France, shares a lot of ingredients with the Mediterranean countries beside her. Thus, the black olives, anchovies, and tomatoes. It has become so familiar and a great favorite of mine that even without a recipe I can tell if an ingredient is missing.

3 pcs. cooked potatoes
100 gms. green beans (habichuelas), cooked and cut into diagonal slices
2 - 4 pcs. firm, red tomatoes, cut into quarter of eights
1 sweet green pepper, diced
Baguio lettuce, clean and crisp, torn into bite-sized pieces
1 cup tuna fish in chunks
1 hard cooked eggs
6 slices anchovy, filets
8 - 10 pcs of black, ripe olives

Cook potatoes, green beans and eggs. Set aside and allow to cool. Prepare bowl with all the vegetables in it. Leave some of the tomatoes for garnishing. Arrange chunks of tuna in the bowl. Mix in the sliced hard cooked eggs. Keep some of the eggs for decor. Arrange the anchovies, black olives and red tomatoes with some green pepper and green beans for color. Chill everything. Just before serving, pour the chilled French dressing and serve.

French Dressing or Vinaigrette

The original vinaigrette uses only oil and vinegar. However, I find that using Dijon mustard with some herbs improves the dressing considerably. So you can add chopped parsley, green onions, chives or estragon to enhance your dressing. Using olive oil or walnut oil changes the personality of the dressing. Substituting calamansi juice or dayap juice for vinegar makes a difference as well.

2 tbsp. *Dijon* **mustard**
1 tbsp. good red vinegar (wine or fruit)
3 - 4 tbsp. salad oil
Salt and freshly ground pepper to taste

Put mustard, salt, pepper and vinegar in a small bowl. Add oil slowly while mixing constantly. Correct seasoning and chill before serving. Shake or mix well before serving.

Note: The above is just about the proportion and amount one needs for serving salad to 5 persons. However, if you want to prepare the dressing ahead of time and keep it for future use, you can just use 1 part mustard, 1 part vinegar, 3 - 4 parts oil. Then add salt and pepper. Keep in a covered bottle and store in the refrigerator. Shake well before using.

Coleslaw

Cabbage is a vegetable that is comparatively inexpensive and is found in our markets the year round. This salad is also found in many eating places, particularly in fastfood restaurants. Here is a recipe I have used for almost all my cooking life.

1 medium cabbage, shredded (about 2 cups)
1 - 2 carrots, shredded (about 3/4 cup)
1/2 cup raisins
1/2 cup pineapple tidbits, drained
1/2 cup chopped peanuts (optional)
1/2 - 3/4 cup mayonnaise

Toss ingredients together.
To the mayonnaise, one can add cream or milk to dilute the mayonnaise as a dressing.
Coleslaw can be made with just sliced cabbage and carrots. But the addition of the other ingredients make a richer more interesting salad.

Caesar Salad

This is one salad that was popularized in the Sixties. It still is a big favorite in restaurants.

1 clove garlic, peeled
1 tbsp. *Dijon* mustard
1 tbsp. lemon juice
2 tbsp. grated Parmesan cheese
2 fillets of anchovies
1 egg yolk
3 tbsp. olive oil
Crisp Baguio lettuce, cut into bite-size pieces
2 tbsp. crisp fried bacon (about 3 slices), chopped into bits
1/2 cup croutons (from 2 to 3 slices of sandwich bread)

Use day-old sandwich bread slices. Cut into cubes and fry in butter. Set aside. Rub the bottom of the salad bowl with the garlic (cut on one end). You may want to add some finely chopped garlic but it is best to use garlic judiciously. Using a wooden spoon, mix in the mustard, the egg yolk, the anchovies and the olive oil. Then blend in the lemon juice. A few drops of Tabasco can be added for tang. Add the torn lettuce leaves and bacon bits and blend carefully with the dressing. Sprinkle Parmesan cheese and croutons and mix. Save some of the croutons for topping. Serve at once.

OSMEÑA

CABEZA DE JABALI
FLAN DE LECHE COCIDO
EN CACEROLA MIRRO MATIC
RICH FRUIT CAKE
ARROZ A LA VALENCIANA
CAMARON REBOSADO
TORTA VISAYA
OSSO BUCO
BACALAO A LA VIZCAINA
COCIDO PORTUGUES

I N MY book, *Annie Osmeña Aboitiz is one outstanding lady. I met her* *years ago when she was still single and visiting a close family friend,* *Doña Isabel Roces. Tita Bebeng Roces had many friends but Annie was* *one of her favorites. I was to learn why during one of my trips to Cebu* *where I researched on food as prepared in this central Visayan island.*

When I visited Annie in her fabulous home, I told her that I was *writing a new cookbook and hoped she would share some of her family* *recipes. Many would rather keep these as secret only to be used by the* *family but Annie gave me all of it, her kitchen files plus old cookbooks* *and notebooks all full of her family's culinary heritage. I was so touched* *by her generosity.*

It would be unthinkable to abuse such generosity and so I chose only *some dishes to include in this cookbook. Much of the personal recipes I* *told Annie would remain secret. She approved of those I had chosen and* *trusted me with the others.*

Most of the recipes here, Annie wrote me later, were from friends of *her maternal grandmother, Eulalia Oriol Renner who had a German* *father and a Spanish mestiza mother. It was to Annie that she gave her* *collection of recipes.*

Two of the recipes printed here are from the original written in *Spanish. The rest are translations.*

Cabeza de Jabali (Receta de Mrs. Jakosalem)

2 piernas de cerdo regular
1 1/2 kilo carne de cerdo con un poco de gordura
6 chorizos de Bilbao
Sweet pickle cortado a lo largo
Sal y pimienta

Se deshuesa la pierna quitando las patitas. Se pica la carne. El chorizo se corta a lo largo en dos. Se tiempla con sal y pimienta la carne. Se espolvorea con sal y pimienta la pierna y se pone la carne entre medio, se insierta el chorizo y el sweet pickle se cierra (la pierna cociendolo y se envuelve en sinamay amarandolo apretadamente y se coce en agua con fuego lento en 2 horas y 1/2, se le quita el sinamay y se envuelve en otra tela, se amarra bien y se pone en la nevera a helar, y se sirve frio.

Flan de Leche Cocido en Cacerola Mirro Matic™

La misma receta de Flan de Leche.

Se pone la mezcla en el molde como los otros flanes y se tapa con wax paper atandolo con un bramante, se coloca en la cacerola donde se ha puesto un poco de agua, lo suficiente para estar al nivel de calzo en el fondo de la misma, se cierra bien y se pone el graduador en el numer 5, y en cuanto empiece hacer el tic, tic, tic, se cuenta 3 minutos y se apaga el fuego dejandolo enfriar. Antes de abrir la cacerola se quita el graduador se saca del molde antes de que se enfrie del todo. Al quitarse del fuego se quita el graduador y se abre la cacerola de ajo.

Note: See next page for English translation.

Cabeza de Jabali
(Receta de Mrs. Jakosalem)

This recipe is a modified version of the Boar's Head which was considered a delicacy. Don Alfonso Calalang talked about it frequently mentioning that the flavor comes from the gamey taste of the head and the gelatinous substances from the skin.

Mrs. Generosa Teves Cui Jakosalem was the wife of Governor Dionisio Jakosalem, Secretary of Commerce and Communication from 1917 to 1922 during the time of Governor Harrison. They belong to one of the oldest families of Cebu.

2 pcs. pig's legs, regular size
1 1/2 kilo pork with little fat, chopped
6 pcs. *chorizo de Bilbao*
Sweet pickles cut into strips
Salt and pepper

Debone the pig's legs. Chop pork and season with salt and pepper. Cut *chorizo* into two lengthwise.

Sprinkle salt and pepper into the pig legs. Stuff legs with chopped pork, chorizos and pickles. Close the legs and wrap in *sinamay*. Fasten securely.

Cook stuffed pig's legs in water for 2 1/2 hours. Remove *sinamay* and wrap in another cloth. Fasten properly. Put in the refrigerator. Serve cold.

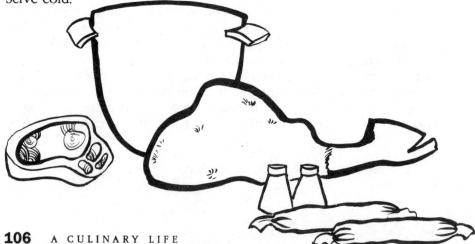

Flan de Leche Cocido en Cacerola Mirro Matic™

This recipe is unique since it is cooked in a pressure cooker whose brand name Mirro Matic™ *is specified in the title. The instructions are also very specific down to the number of "tics" one has to count while the flan is cooking.*

The recipe for the leche flan *is taken from one of my cookbooks.*

Leche flan
 1 1/4 cups evaporated milk
 3/4 cups water
 8 egg yolks
 1 tsp. lemon rind or vanilla
 1/2 cup caramel syrup *

Scald the evaporated milk and water in double-boiler for 15 minutes. Beat egg yolks. Add sugar, milk and flavoring. Pour into 1 quart mold.

*Caramelized syrup

 1 cup sugar
 1/2 cup hot water

Melt sugar in heavy metal container. As soon as sugar is golden brown, add 1/2 cup hot water to dissolve caramelized sugar and form syrup.

Put the mixture in a mold and cover with wax paper fastened with a cord.

Place the mold in the pressure cooker. Put enough water to submerge the bottom of the mold. Cover well and put gauge in #5. When it starts to "tic tic tic", count 3 minutes and remove pressure cooker from the stove. Leave it to cool. Before opening the pressure cooker, remember to remove the gauge.

Rich Fruit Cake
(Receta de Amparing)

Amparing Palacio was the wife of Manuel Palacio who was manager of Elizalde and Co. for almost three decades, from 1936 to 1964.

1 pack big raisins
1/4 kilo dried lemon
1/4 kilo nuts
1 lemon (juice and peel needed)
1/2 pack dates
2 cups butter
1/2 cup brandy
2 cups brown sugar
6 eggs
4 cups flour
4 tbsp. baking powder
2 tbsp. cinnamon
1/2 tsp. nutmeg, allspices
1 small bottle grape juice (about 3/4 cup)

A day before, cut the fruits and soak in grape juice. The following day, mix the fruits and lemon juice, peel and rind.

Cream butter. Add eggs one at a time mixing continuously. Add sifted flour mixed with baking powder. Add the fruits and the spices.

Put into a mold and bake at 325 degrees F.

Arroz a la Valenciana
de Nik Osmeña

Clams
Crab
Shrimps
Squid
Tanguingue
Rice from Valencia (Spain), washed
Garlic, mascerated
Onions, finely chopped
Olive oil
Pimenton
Saffron
Salt
Pepper

Boil clams, crab and shrimps and reserve broth. Shell the shrimps but leave the head intact.

Clean squid and remove its ink sac. Cut the squid crosswise thus forming circles. Keep the head and tentacles whole.

In another pan, fry some olive oil and fry squid. As you remove the squid, add a few drops of soy sauce on the pieces.

Fry tanguigue that has been cut into pieces.

Fry garlic in olive oil until golden brown. Then add the Valencia rice that has been washed. Some of the pimenton and saffron is added to the washed rice. Continue cooking for five minutes and then remove from the flame.

In another open pan, fry the rest of the garlic with all the chopped onions. Add the rice mixture. Add salt and pepper. Add the sea food broth in the proportion of 2 cups of stock for every cup of rice. Spread banana leaves on top and cover with the tight-fitting lid and cook for 25 minutes allowing the fried fish, clams and crab (cut into two) to be encrusted in the rice. The pieces of squid and shrimps are arranged on top.

When the rice is almost done, the pan is transferred to the oven set at moderate heat. Continue cooking the rice until it is done. Serve hot.

Camaron Rebosado
(Receta de Tere Fortich)

Tere Fortich is the daughter of Congresswoman Remedios Ozamiz Fortich from Bukidnon whose own version of the Salsa Monja is also featured in this cookbook.

4 eggs
4 pcs. green onions
1 cup shrimps, shelled and cleaned
Salt
1 tbsp. flour with a pinch of baking powder
2 tbsp. cooking oil

Chop green onions and fry in cooking oil. Beat eggs until lemon-colored. Add flour with baking powder. Add shrimps into flour and add salt to taste. Plut a spoonful into frying pan with enough oil. Fry until brown.

Torta Visaya

5 cups flour
1 cup *tuba*
3 cups sugar
20 eggs (yolk only)
1 1/2 cups cooking oil
1/4 tsp. salt
A pinch of anise

Pour the *tuba* into the flour. Add the salt. Mix well.
Add the sugar gradually into the egg yolks while beating well. Add the oil and put into a pan lined with paper and greased with butter or oil. Add anise. Wait for 7 hours before baking (to allow the batter to rise). However if the weather is cold, wait for 8 hours before baking.
Bake at 325°F.

Osso Buco

1/2 cup butter
1 big onion, chopped to measure 3/4 cup
1 big carrot, chopped
1/2 cup chopped celery
2 tsp. minced garlic
2 kilos beef shank — choose meaty part and sawn across to
yield 5 to 6 pcs., 2 inches thick. Dredge in salt and pepper and
1/2 cup flour.
1/2 cup oil
3/4 cup dry white wine or water
1 tbsp. salt plus 1 tsp. salt
1/2 tsp. thyme
1 tsp. pepper
1 big can whole tomatoes
6 parsley sprigs
2 bay leaves

In a pressure cooker, saute onion in butter, then add carrots, celery
and garlic. Set aside.

In a frying pan, add the oil and brown beef on both sides. Transfer
beef to pressure cooker and add all ingredients and 1 cup water, bones
and cook for 40 minutes, or till beef is tender. Do not open pressure
cooker until it cools (or when pressure valve goes down).

An ordinary pot can be used for boiling but use 5 cups of water
instead to soften the shank.

Bacalao a la Vizcaina

1 kilo bacalao
1/2 kilo onions, cut in strips
1/2 kilo onions, chopped
1 kilo tomato, chopped
6 pimientos
2 cloves garlic
1/2 kilo tomato, chopped
olive oil
a few teaspoons of breadcrumbs

Soak the bacalao in water overnight. Throw the water the next day. Place the bacalao in a pan and pour cold water. Heat the pan and wait until the water starts to boil. Remove pan from the fire as it starts to boil. Take the bacalao and remove bones carefully so that the fish does not crumble. Dredge the bacalao with a little flour and fry with olive oil.

In the same oil, saute the onions that are cut in strips and 1 kilo chopped tomato. This will serve as the first sauce.

In a separate pan, fry the garlic, the chopped onions, the 1/2 kilo chopped tomato and pimientos that have been passed through a sieve. This serves as the second sauce.

Add the first sauce to the second sauce. In an earthenware or pyrex dish put 1 layer of sauce then a layer of bacalao. Continue with the layers but make sure the last layer is the sauce. Over that, add the broiled pimientos that have been peeled and cut in strips. Spread a few bread crumbs and a little garlic and bake for 20 to 30 minutes.

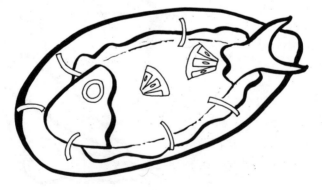

Cocido Portugues

1 large chicken, cut into pieces
2 pcs. pig's legs, small size
1/4 kilo Chinese sausage, cut into pieces
150 grams Chinese ham
1 1/2 kilo cabbage
1 kilo pechay
1 onion, chopped
2 tbsp. lard

Boil to soften pig's legs, debone and cut into pieces. Set meat and broth aside.

Saute onion in lard. Add cut chicken. Fry a little. Add 5 glasses of water and the ham. Cook.

Once the chicken has softened, add the sausage, vegetables, pig's legs and the broth. Cook only for 20 minutes so as not to overcook the vegetables.

Serve with *bagoong* sauteed in tomatoes, onions and pork.

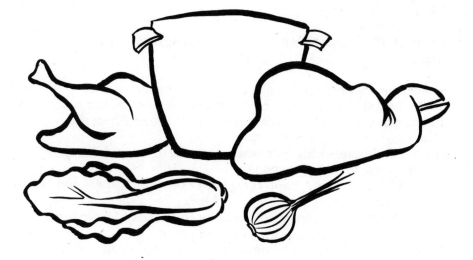

Pasta Putanesca

This popular pasta sauce was prepared by Isabel, the talented daughter of my hosts in Washington D.C., Mr. and Mrs. Benito Legarda Jr. Isabel is the granddaughter of Dr. Guadalupe Fores Ganzon, a professor of the University of the Philippines when I was a student there. I remember her fondly and used to call her Magan (for Mama Ganzon). It was she who prompted me to take Home Economics when I was unsure what course to pursue at the university.

1 1/2 - 2 cups *pancetta* (slab bacon), cut in cubes
1 1/2 cups - 2 cups chopped white onions
1/3 cup finely chopped garlic
8 whole tomatoes (medium), peeled, seeded and chopped
1/2 cup finely chopped parsley
1 tsp. red pepper flakes
6 tbsps. capers
18 whole black olive, pitted
12 pcs. anchovies, drained and chopped coarsley
2 tbsp. tomato paste
3 tbsp. basil
3 tsp. oregano
1 cup olive oil
1 can of 385 gms. (about 1 1/2 cups) spaghetti sauce
sugar

Simmer *pancetta* cubes in cold water for 5 minutes. Drain.

Heat olive oil and cook garlic till soft but not brown. Add onions and pancetta. Cook till soft over medium heat. (Adjust heat if it gets too hot.)

Mix tomato paste with a little water and add to the pot. Stir and cook 3 minutes, then add tomatoes.

Add 1/2 of the parsley, basil, oregano, red pepper, capers and black olives. Stir frequently.

Thicken with canned spaghetti sauce or the juice of whole tomatoes. Add sugar until the sauce is no longer sour.

Cook 25 minutes. Remove from fire. Slice olives in half and return to sauce.

Before serving, add anchovies and remaining parsley. Stir well one minute over medium heat.

VEGETABLE

PINAKBET
AMPALAYA BRAISED WITH BEEF
FRESH LUMPIA
LUMPIA UBOD
LUMPIA WITH MONGO SPROUTS
DINENDENG, LASWA, BULANGLANG
GULAY NA MAIS
GUISADONG GULAY
STUFFED SWEET PEPPER
MONGO GUISADO
GADO GADO
ADOBONG KANGKONG
RADISH PICKLES
CHAYOTE MIXED PICKLES

THE QUALITY and quantity of fruits and vegetables found in the Philippines I believe has deteriorated. Many farms in the countryside have been left unattended because of two things; unrest in the countryside and migration of families to the cities to look for higher-paying jobs. Most of the younger generation also do not find living in the countryside pleasant or challenging.

A farmer in Batangas has told me that he avoids planting vegetables and fruits because it only leads to fights. When the plant is ready for harvest, some teenagers swarm over the land to pick the fruits or vegetables. Trying to defend his property only gets him into fights. He feels that there is no more respect for property.

One man's reason for stopping multiplied by the number of communities in the country explains the low supply and ragged look of our fruits and vegetables. The poor fruits were probably picked in a kind of race between the one who grew the fruit and those who raid farms as a pastime, a shameless way of living off the work of others.

Pinakbet

My sister-in-law, Tessie Villegas Daza, received this **pinakbet** *as a gift from her sister, Fe Villegas Baclig, and shared it with me. It was the best* pinakbet *I had ever tasted. The small eggplants were bursting with flavor and yet were so tender they almost melted in the mouth.*

The Bacligs are from Ilocos and have kept this recipe as part of their family treasure. I pestered Tessie until I got the recipe. Virginia Baclig Sevalla gallantly shared this recipe with hints on how to ensure success. The main thing, of course, is to use the best fish bagoong *from the North, be it from the Ilocos or Pangasinan.*

For non-Ilocanos who may not be addicted to "bagoong", Virginia has added tomato sauce.

1/2 kilo pork *liempo* or 350 grams Ilocano *bagnet*
1 kilo small eggplants
1/4 kilo small *ampalaya*
1/4 kilo tomatoes
2 large onions, sliced
1/3 cup tomato sauce
1/2 cup water
1/3 cup fish *bagoong*

(If one is using pork *liempo*, prepare as if for lechon kawali. Be sure to fry till skin is dark golden brown [not black] and crisp.)

Cut the cooked pork or *bagnet* into finger-like pieces. Slice onions and tomatoes and line the bottom of a heavy pan with these. The eggplants should be whole but pricked at random with an ice pick. (Since the recipe is as good as it is, I used an ice pick too!) Cut the *ampalaya* into halves, lengthwise (you may want to discard the seeds). Arrange vegetables and pork in layers over the sliced onions and tomatoes. Pour in tomato sauce and water. Cook in tightly covered pan until eggplants turn brown. Carefully pour off the liquid and dilute the fish *bagoong* with the liquid from the cooked vegetables. Strain the mixture back into the cooking pan. Cook this covered until the vegetables are cooked. Occasionally toss vegetables in the pan to prevent them from sticking. DO NOT MIX WITH SPOON OR FORK. Correct seasoning and serve.

Ampalaya Braised with Beef

1/2 kilo *ampalaya* or amargoso
200 gms. beef tenderloin, sliced thin
2 tbsp. black *tausi*
1/2 tsp. sugar
1 clove garlic, crushed
2 tbsp. soy sauce
2 tbsp. rice wine
3/4 cup stock
1 tsp. cornstarch

Split *ampalaya*. Remove seeds and scrape white membrane. Parboil for 3 minutes, then drain. Slice thinly, and set aside.

Wash *tausi*, drain, then mash together with garlic.

Heat oil in pan, add mashed *tausi* and stir for 1/2 minutes. Drop ampalaya and saute 2 minutes. Add the beef and saute 1 minute. Season with soy sauce, sugar and wine. Pour in the stock. Braise for 1 minute. Thicken with cornstarch. Cook and serve.

Fresh Lumpia

3 tbsp. cooking oil
1 tbsp *achuete* (annatto seeds)
2 tbsp. fat
2 cloves garlic
1/2 cup onion, chopped
1/4 kilo pork, boiled and cut into thin slices
200 gms. shrimps, shelled
3/4 cup shrimp juice*
3/4 cup pork stock
1 cup yellow *camote*, cubed
1 cup potatoes, cubed
3 cups cabbage, shredded
2 cups string beans, cut in strips
1 cup *garbanzos*, cooked

1/4 cup *kinchay*, cut in strips
4 pcs. *tokwa* (soybean curd)
1 tsp. salt
2 tbsp. *patis* (fish sauce)
20 pcs. lettuce leaves
20 pcs. *lumpia* wrapper

Soak *achuete* in 3 tbsp. cooking oil. Set aside.

Saute garlic in 2 tbsp. fat until light brown. Add onions, pork and shrimps. Pour in water of soup stock and cover. Cook over medium heat until pork is tender. Add *camote*, potatoes and cook for 5 minutes. Mix in the rest of the vegetables.

Strain *achuete*-oil to the vegetable mixture. Season with salt and *patis*. Cook until all vegetables are done. Cool in a colander while allowing liquid to drain out. When cool, wrap in *lumpia* wrapper with a leaf of lettuce showing at one end. Serve with brown sauce.

Brown Sauce:

1/2 cup sugar
1 tbsp. soy sauce
2 cups broth
1 tsp. salt
2 tbsp. cornstarch dispersed in 1/4 cup water
4 - 6 cloves garlic, minced

Blend first 4 ingredients together. Bring to boil. Remove from fire. Thicken with cornstarch. Sprinkle with minced garlic and serve.

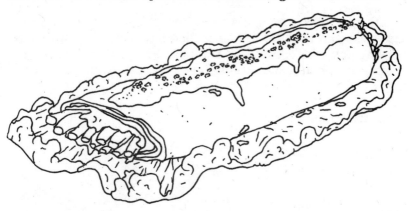

Lumpia Ubod

2 tbsp. cooking oil
2 cloves garlic, crushed
1 small onion, chopped
1/4 cup cooked ham, chopped
1/4 kilo boiled pork, diced
1/2 cup shrimps, chopped
1/2 cup cooked *garbanzos* or chick peas
1 cup snap beans or *habichuelas*, cut into diagonal strips
1/2 kilo *ubod* or heart of palm, cut into match-like strips
2 cups cabbage, shredded
2 tsp. salt
24 pcs. lettuce leaves or spring onions
1 cup carrots, julienne

Brown garlic in hot cooking oil. Add onions and cook slowly until soft. Add the pork, ham, shrimps and *garbanzos*. Simmer for 5 minutes. Combine carrots, stringbeans and ubod. Cook covered until vegetables are half-done. Drop the cabbage and continue cooking until done. Drain and season. Cool. Set broth aside for Brown Sauce.* Wrap mixture in home-made wrapper lined with lettuce leaves or spring onions. Serve with Brown Sauce.

Home-made lumpia wrapper

2 duck eggs
1/2 cup cornstarch dispersed in 1 cup water

Separate egg yolks from egg whites. Beat egg whites until frothy. Add egg yolks and beat just to blend. Blend in dispersed cornstarch. Brush frying pan with cooking oil and heat. Spoon about 2 tbsp. batter, then tilt pan to spread batter evenly on pan. Lift off wrapper when done.

*Brown sauce recipe on page 119.

Lumpia with Mongo Sprouts

2 tbsp. oil
3 cloves garlic, minced
2 medium-sized onions, chopped
1/4 kilo ground pork
1/4 kilo shrimps, chopped
1/2 kilo mongo sprouts, clean and remove brown tips
2 cups cabbage, shredded finely
1 cup green beans, cut into small pieces
1/2 up carrots, shredded
1 - 2 tbsp. soy sauce
50 pcs. *lumpia* wrappers
fresh lettuce leaves
ground peanuts

Saute the garlic, onions and ground pork. Cook till pork is done. Add chopped shrimps. Add the mongo sprouts, cabbage, green beans and carrots. Season with soy sauce. When vegetables are cooked, drain out all liquid. Wrap vegetable mixture in *lumpia* wrappers with lettuce leaves showing in one end. Sprinkle ground peanuts on top of vegetable mixture before wrapping. Serve with sauce.

Sauce: (Paalat)

1/4 cup brown sugar
1/4 cup soy sauce
1/2 cup water
3 tbsp. cornstarch in 1/4 cup water
3 cloves freshly pounded garlic

Dissolve sugar in soy sauce and water over low flame. Add the cornstarch dispersed in water. Let boil till it thickens. Add the garlic last.

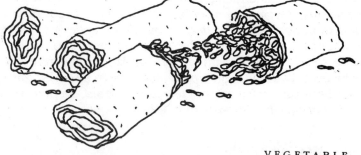

Dinendeng, Laswa, Bulanglang

These vegetables dishes can be taken to be one and the same. It is made up of fresh vegetables and in the provinces this usually means whatever is available in one's backyard. The dish is called **dinendeng** *in Northern Luzon,* laswa *in Iloilo and* bulanglang *in the Tagalog regions. It is basically a vegetable dish cooked in rice washing and spiced with either or all of garlic, onions, ginger. Flavoring is with fish* bagoong *or* patis *(fish sauce). Sometimes broiled fish or pork is added.*

When I asked some Iloilo ladies their recipe of laswa, *they looked at me as if I had asked them to teach me how to walk. It is a dish they grew up with and they thought that preparing it should come naturally.*

This dish is not easily duplicated in cities where vegetables travel a long way from provincial sources. But in most rural areas, the vegetables are picked from the family backyard and when cooked has a sweetish taste—a simple dish yet a perfect masterpiece in culinary art.

Dinendeng *is best eaten right after cooking and cooking it doesn't take that long. Its secret, as with most Ilocano food, is in the* bagoong *made of fermented* munamon *(dilis). The procedure is quite simple. Water to which the* bagoong *is added is boiled.* Camote *in cubes is then added for its sweet taste. After which the vegetables are thrown in. Ilocanos will say that any available vegetable will do. What is important is not to cover the* dinendeng *while cooking to preserve the color of the vegetables and prevent overcooking. It is a simple food with a lot of flavor and rather healthy at that. Up north,* dinendeng *is breakfast food.*

Another version of the dinendeng *uses the* malunggay *pods. The* bagoong *should be strained first then boiled for some time to take away the fishy taste. The* malunggay *pods also have to be boiled for some ten minutes because it takes a long time to be cooked. Properly done, the pods will have a sweetish taste to it.* **MF** *daing* (*dalag* about 100-150 gms.)

1/4 k. chayote, sliced
2 *calabasa*
2 large tomatoes cut into quarters
1 cup *sitao* cut to 1 1/2" lengths
1 1/2 to 2 tbsp. *bagoong*
1 cup rice washing
1/4 tsp. msg

Broil the *daing* and cut into quarters. Mix all the above ingredients except the leaves. Cover and cook for about ten minutes. Add leafy vegetables and cook for about 5 to 10 minutes more. Add seasoning (correct according to taste) and serve hot. Serves 4.

Gulay na Mais

2 tbsp. cooking oil
3 cloves garlic, crushed
1 onion, sliced thin
1/4 kilo shrimps. sliced
2 cups shrimp stock
1 cup young corn, slice from cob and then scrape
2 tsp. *patis*
1/8 cup pepper leaves (*sili* leaves)
dash of pepper

Saute garlic. When golden brown, add onions and shrimps. Add shrimp stock and bring to a boil. Add scraped corn and simmer until the corn is cooked. Add seasonings. Add green pepper leaves and continue cooking for 3 minutes before removing from fire. Serve hot.

Guisadong Gulay

2 tbsp. cooking oil
4 cloves garlic, crushed
1 medium-sized onion, sliced
2 medium-sized tomatoes, sliced
1/2 cup shrimps, shelled and diced
1/2 cup pork belly, boiled and cut into strips
3 tbsp. *patis* (fish sauce)
1/2 cup shrimp juice (pound head and shell mixed with small
amount of water then strain to get juice)
1/4 kilo Baguio beans, cut diagonally into 1 1/2 inches long
1/4 kilo carrots, cut into strips
1/2 kilo cabbage, shredded,
salt to taste

Heat the oil in a skillet, then saute the garlic until light brown. Add
the onions and cook until transparent. Add the tomatoes and continue
mixing until mushy. Lastly, add the pork and shrimps. Season with fish
sauce. Correct seasoning. Add shrimp juice and bring to a boil Add
carrots, cover and cook for 5 minutes. Add Baguio beans and cook for
2 minutes. Add cabbage last and cook till done.

Stuffed Sweet Pepper or
Eggplants (rellenong talong)

4 red or green sweet pepper (*siling* Baguio)
3 cloves garlic, macerated
5 tbsp. oil
1 large onion, chopped
2 tomatoes, chopped
1/4 - 1/2 cup pork stock
1/2 kilo ground pork
salt and pepper
2 eggs beaten, seasoned with
salt and pepper

Boil sweet pepper. Set aside.

Saute garlic, onion, tomatoes and ground pork in hot fat. Add stock. Season with salt and pepper. When done, remove from fire and cool.

Mix part of beaten egg with meat mixture. Remove top portion of sweet pepper and fill with meat mixture.

Eggplant:

Boil or broil eggplant. Peel. Split and spread fan like. Top with cooked ground pork and spread over surface. Dip into beaten eggs covering eggplant and ground pork. Lay stuffed eggplant into hot oil and fry till top is golden brown.

Mongo Guisado
Balatong

1 cup green mongo, boiled in
3 cups water
1 tbsp. cooking oil
2 cloves garlic, crushed
1 onion, chopped
6 tomatoes, chopped
1/2 cup pork, boiled and sliced into strips
1/2 cup shrimps, peeled and sliced
2 tbsp. *bagoong*
4 cups water or broth
1 tsp. salt
1 cup *sitsaron* or crackling, cut into pieces

Boil mongo until soft. Rub through a fine sieve or puree. Set aside.

Saute garlic, onion and tomatoes in oil. Drop pork and shrimps. Cook 1 minute. Add *bagoong* and mongo. Pour water and simmer, season with salt. Just before taking out from the fire, add cracklings. Serve hot.

Gado-gado

100 grams cabbage
100 grams Baguio beans
100 grams carrots
100 grams cauliflower
150 grams *togue*
1 cucumber
2 medium potatoes
2 square *tokwa*, fried until light brown, then cubed

Wash and clean all the vegetables.
Boil water in a big pan and add a little salt. Blanch the vegetables one at a time. Strain.
Arrange the vegetables and *tokwa* on a platter.

Peanut sauce:

3 tbsp. oil
4-5 cloves garlic, minced
1/2 cup *sibuyas tagalog*, minced
1/4 cup *bagoong alamang*
1 siling *haba*, sliced
2-3 tbsp. brown sugar
1/4 cup tamarind juice
3/4 cup peanut butter
1 coconut (*niyog*) grated—add 1/2 cup water to obtain 2 cups coco milk

Heat oil. Saute garlic and *sibuyas tagalog*. Add *bagoong*, *sili*, sugar and tamarind juice. Mix in peanut butter and coco milk.
Correct seasoning. Serve with the above vegetables.

Adobong Kangkong

400 grams or 2 bundles of *kangkong*
1/4 cup water
1/4 cup vinegar
1/2 cup pork, diced
3 tbsp. *patis*
4 cloves garlic, crushed
1 onion, chopped
1 tsp. pepper

Wash and parboil the *kangkong* in water. Set aside. Fry the pork. Push to one side of the pan. Saute garlic, onion and *kangkong*. Season with vinegar, *patis* and pepper. Cook until kangkong is tender crisp.

Note: Substitutes for *kangkong* may be: okra, *sitao* and *puso ng saging* (banana heart).

Radish pickles

1 radish
3 tbsp. rock salt
2 tbsp. vinegar
1/2 tsp. sesame oil
3 tbsp. sugar
1 red pepper, sliced thin

Peel skin of radish thickly and slice paper-thin. Add rock salt, press down and let stand 2 to 3 hours or overnight. Rinse with water until no longer salty. Squeeze out water. Add vinegar, sesame oil, sugar and red pepper.

Chayote mixed pickles

(achara)

1 1/2 k. *chayote*, cut in 1" strips
2 regular-sized carrots, cut in strips
20 pcs. *sibuyas* **Tagalog or shallots**
1 sweet red pepper, the thick variety
1 green pepper, the thick variety
1 small pc. ginger (about 2")

Wash, peel and cut the vegetables into long thin strips. Work the vegetables individually with salt and press to remove juice. Mix all the vegetables and pack in clean dry container. Prepare the pickle solution.

Pickle solution:

2 cups native vinegar
1 1/2 cups sugar
2 tbsp. salt

Boil solution. Strain and pour over the vegetables. Pack in jars. Remove air bubbles by inserting a knife around the side of the bottle. Fill up with more pickle solution. Cover tightly.

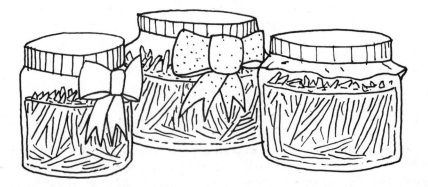

DESSERT

BICOL PILI NUT PIE
SANS RIVAL
LE GATEAU DE SANS RIVAL
PRUNE CAKE
BLITZ TORTE
BRAZO DE MERCEDES
BUKO PIE
CANONIGO
CHOCOLATE CRINKLES
LEMON SQUARES
ELEGANT MOUSSE TORTE
CHOCOLATE CREAM CHEESE CAKE
SPRITZ COOKIES
MANGO CAKE

I BELIEVE THAT of all the countries in Southeast Asia, the desserts of the Philippines are the most varied. They include the flans, pastillas and natillas of Spain as well as the pies, cakes, jams, jellies, ice cream and sherbets of the United States.

Many Filipinos who have settled in other Asian countries own bake shops that are successful. One of them is my partner at Mai Thai, Sylvia Cancio Lim who began a shop in Malaysia that is still doing well. The top pastry and bakery in Thailand is owned by Nene Sirisampan, a Filipina who has settled in Bangkok. Her sister, Mrs. Dominador Ambrosio began the "Bahay Kubo ni Ligaya" in the late Thirties which later became the renowned Country Bakeshop. This was where I tasted for the first time what I consider still the best mocca cake. They served a variety of exceptional pastries such as cinammon rolls, chocolate cake, and chocolate beehive. They also introduced silvanas that have become so popular in today's bake shops.

Bicol Pili Nut Pie

2 cups all-purpose flour
1 tbsp. sugar
1 tsp. baking powder
1/2 cup fat or shortening
1 tbsp. margarine
4 - 5 tbsp. cold water

Pastry shell:

Combine flour, sugar, and baking powder in a bowl. Cut in shortening and margarine. Add in beaten egg, tossing to blend. Add water to moisten. Roll mixture on a floured board till about 1/4 inch thick. Place on pie shell. Trim edges.

Filling:

1/2 cup butter
1/2 cup sugar
1/4 cup all-purpose flour
1/4 tsp. salt
3 egg yolks
1/2 cup evaporated milk
1 tsp. vanilla
1/2 cup chopped *pili* nuts

Cream butter and sugar until light and fluffy. Add flour, salt and egg yolks. Mix thoroughly. Stir in evaporated milk and vanilla. Pour into prepared pastry shell and sprinkle *pili* nuts on top. Bake at 425°F for 10 minutes. Reduce heat to 300°F and continue baking until filling is cooked (approximately 40 minutes.)

Sans Rival

Food like clothes go through periods when they are "in." It was egg pie in the Forties and Fifties, sold in many Chinese bakeries in Carriedo. In the Sixties and Seventies, it was **Sans Rival.**

When I introduced the dish in my restaurant in Paris in 1973, I called it Gateau Manille *and used almonds instead of cashew nuts. The French never suspected that the dessert originated in Paris. As a matter of fact,* Sans Rival *is included in a cookbook by the* Ecole de Cordon Bleu *published in 1895.*

There must have been a select group of Filipinas who went to Paris and took courses at the Cordon Bleu. They must have shared this recipe with others in Manila which, I believe, was how Sans Rival *was introduced to the country.*

Due to the intricate and complicated way the original Sans Rival *was made, it is no longer prepared in Paris (although Gaston Lenotre is reviving old desserts and cakes and has come up with something similar using several layers of* meringue *and praline). But here,* Sans Rival *is available to us in most bakeshops.*

The following recipe is a simpler one. I sometimes make variations like adding Grand Maniere to the yolk mixture instead of rum and sprinkling the top with crumbled meringue.

Sans Rival *is best stored in a freezer and served immediately after it has slightly defrosted. The* meringue *should remain crisp and dry.*

---

6 egg whites
3/4 c. sugar
1-1/2 cashew nuts, chopped finely
1 tsp. vanilla

Grease and flour heavily 3 inverted 18-inch x 15-inch cookie sheets. Set aside.

Beat egg whites until soft peaks are formed. Gradually add the sugar, beating well after each addition. Continue beating until the egg whites are stiff. Fold in cashew nuts and vanilla. Spread thinly in prepared pans. Bake at 300°F for 20 minutes or until golden brown. Cut wafers in the center if desired. Loosen and slide wafers to a flat surface. Cool. (Work while wafers are hot because they are hard to loosen as they are crisp when cool.) Prepare filling.

Filling:
  1 cup sugar
  1/3 cup water
  6 egg yolks
  1/2 lb. butter
  2 tbsp. rum

Boil sugar and water until it spins a thread. Meanwhile, beat egg yolks in thin streams while beating. Cool. Cream butter. Blend in the egg yolk mixture and rum. Fill and cover wafers with filling. Sprinkle top with chopped cashew nuts. Serve chilled.

Classic Cake

Sans Rival. No need to bother with French and translations when you hear those two words. Instead, visions of a cake, not quite like any cake, comes into mind. Layers of thin wafer held together by the creamiest of butter icing with a sprinkling of chopped cashew nuts on top of the final icing layer.

No need to know French either to pronounce sans rival correctly. The spelling and words have no inherent difficulty unlike *meringue* which always ends up sounding provincial (me-reng-gue) on non-French tongues.

But if you know that sans rival in English means "without rival," it would merely confirm what every bakeshop habitue here has known— that among the pastries, it is the one that inspires awe, demands respect and deserves the high price attached to it.

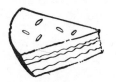

Even if it has become a regular item in bake shops, it has never been regarded as common as chocolate cake. There are neo-cakes with inventive names as exotic as Tobleron, as native as *Pandan* and as surprising as Guava, but these come and go. Sans rival, however, is a classic. **MF**

Le Gateau de Sans Rival

For those who would rather make Sans Rival the Cordon Bleu way, here is the recipe as translated from the French original.

Beat the egg whites of 5 eggs and add delicately with the aid of a spatula, 200 gms. of sugar in powdered form mixed with 200 gms. of grilled almonds that have been chopped finely.

Butter and flour a baking sheet and spread the beaten egg white mixture into four rectangular layers of about 1 cm. thickness. Cook this in a moderate oven. As soon as these are cooked, remove from the sheets and allow to cool on grills.

Prepare a syrup in a saucepan by adding 50 gms of sugar, 50 gms. of hazelnuts that have been toasted and peeled until the hazelnuts turn golden brown and pour the caramel with hazelnuts onto an oiled marble surface to cool. Meantime, add 100 gms. of sugar to a casserole, half a bean of vanilla, 4 tbsps. of water. Cook till it forms a fine thread. Pour this into a bowl with 5 egg yolks and beat well until the mixture cools. Chop the praline made of caramel and hazelnut and add this to the yolk mixture. Keep this *"Creme Mousline au praline"* (the beaten yolks with chopped caramel and hazelnuts) in a cool place.

An almond paste is prepared of 60 gms. of almond, peeled and chopped very finely. Add a few drops of cold water to prevent the almonds from forming oil. In another casserole, prepare syrup with 150 gms. of sugar and cook until the sugar melts then add this to the powdered almonds mix and pound all of it to make something of a *masapan.* Color with a drop of green and mix thoroughly.

To assemble. Cut the edges of the four *meringue* layers to obtain equal sizes. Spread over *meringue* layers a coat of creme mousseline praline. Over the top layer, spread a thin coat of creme mousseline praline and spread the *masapan* of almonds equally over the top.

With a pate of almonds and powdered sugar form a ribbon to arrange on the cake. Make the ribbon with several pieces of almond paste. Prepare a "glace royale" with powdered sugar, a few drops of lemon. With the "glace" paste the ribbon so that it will be held in place. Add a few drops of red food coloring to have a pink icing and pipe out the words *"Sans Rival"* on the ribbons.

Prune Cake

1/2 cup evaporated milk
1/4 cup water
1 tsp. *calamansi* or lemon juice
1 cup prunes
1/4 cup water
1 butter or magarine
1 cup sugar
4 egg yolks
2 1/2 cup sifted cake flour
1 tsp. baking soda
1 tsp. baking powder
4 egg whites
1/2 cup sugar

Combine evaporated milk, water and *calamansi* juice. Let stand until milk coagulates. Boil prunes in water until soft. Pit, then chop. Set aside. Cream butter until light and fluffy. Gradually add sugar, beat until stiff but not dry. Fold into prune mixture. Pour into a paper-lined 13" rectangular pan and bake at 350°F. for 35 - 40 minutes or until done. Cool and split cake. Fill cut layer with prune butter icing. Replace top and frost side and top with prune butter icing.

Prune Butter Icing

Prepare Butter Icing.* Set aside 1/4 cup, add 2/3 cup chopped prunes to remaining icing. Use to fill and frost cake. Decorate with remaining 1/4 cup butter icing.

* Butter Icing:
3/4 cup sugar
1 cup butter
3/4 cup evaporated milk

Dissolve sugar in evaporated milk. Set aside. Cream butter until light and fluffy. Pour sugar-milk mixture in thin streams beating continuously until well blended.

(To shorten creaming time, use 1 cup powdered sugar instead of granulated sugar.)

Blitz Torte

This is an American dessert although its name is German. It is a delicious cake, slightly different and yet very easy to make. This is one of my favorite desserts.

1/2 cup butter
1/2 cup sugar
4 egg yolks
1 tsp. vanilla
2 cups sifted cake flour
1 tsp. baking powder
3 tbsps. evaporated milk
4 egg whites
3/4 cup sugar
1/2 cup chopped cashew or walnuts

Preheat oven to 350°F. Line bottom and sides of 2 8-inch layer pans; extend paper beyond sides of pan. Cream butter until light. Gradually add the sugar and egg yolks beating well. After each addition, blend in the vanilla. Sift flour and baking powder together. Beat in flour-baking powder mixture with evaporated milk beginning and ending with the flour mixture. Pour into prepared pans. Set aside.

Beat 4 eggwhites. Add sugar and beat until stiff peaks are formed. Pile on to the batter. Sprinkle with cinnamon and cashew nuts. Bake at 350°F for 15 minutes or until meringue is set. While waiting for the batter and meringue to be done, prepare cream filling.

Cream Filling:

1/2 cup sugar
1/3 cup all-purpose flour
1/2 tsp. salt
2 cups evaporated milk
2 eggs yolks, slightly beaten
1 tsp. vanilla

Mix sugar, flour and salt insaucepan. Blend in evaporated milk. Cook over medium heat, stirring until the mixture boils. Boil for 10 minutes. Remove from fire. Stir half of cream mixture into egg yolks.

Pour back in sauce pan and blend. Lower heat and cook stirring for 2 minutes more or until mixture coats spoon. Cool and add vanilla.

Spread cream filling on top of one cake-meringue layer and place the other cake-meringue layer on top of that.

Brazo de Mercedes

As the name implies, this dessert must have been brought here by the Spanish. When I served this dessert in Paris, no one commented that it was "Occidental," much less Spanish. It may no longer be served in Spain but it is definitely a part of our repertoire of pastries.

10 egg whites
1 tsp. cream of tartar
1 c. sugar
1 teaspoon vanilla
10 egg yolks
1 can condensed milk

Beat egg whites with cream of tartar till soft peaks form. Add sugar little by little, beating continuously till stiff; add vanilla.

Spread *meringue* onto lined and greased brazo pan or jelly pan. Bake at 250°F for one hour. Prepare filling.

In a double boiler, combine yolks and condensed milk. Stir continously and cook till thick enough to be spread; set aside. Invert baked *meringue* on a piece of brown paper sprinkled with confectioner's sugar. Remove clinging wax paper and spread yolk-condensed milk mixture. Roll as for jelly roll. Slice and serve.

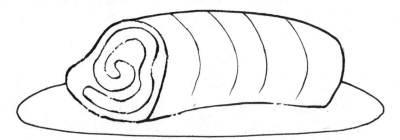

Buko Pie

*When **buko pie** first made its appearance as a tourist buy in Los Baños, Laguna, my sister-in-law, journalist Jullie Yap Daza asked a vender where she learned to bake the pie. To her surprise, the vender answered: "from Nora Daza's cookbook."*

I picked up this recipe from the Home Economics department of the University of the Philippines where I studied and taught and then worked in the Food Service operations from 1952 to 1955.

For the Double Crust Pie:
2 cups all purpose flour
1 tsp. salt
1/3 cup margarine or butter
1/3 cup shortening
3 to 4 tbsp. cold water

Using two knives, cut shortening and butter or margarine into the flour and salt mixture. Cut until the pieces are about the size of peas. Moisten with cold water and gather into a ball. Divide into two parts. Roll out the dough to fit the bottom of the pie plate. Reserve the other for the top.

Buko Filling:
2 cups *buko* meat, scraped
3/4 cup sugar
1/2 evaporated milk
1/2 cornstarch dispersed in
1/2 cup *buko* water

Mix all the ingredients in a saucepan. Cook, stirring constantly until thick. Pour into pastry lined pan. Top with a second crust and bake at 400°F until top is golden brown. Top crust should be perforated with holes to allow steam to escape while baking. Serve cold.

Canonigo

This is a dessert that was taught me by the chef of New Europe, a top restaurant in the early Fifties and Sixties. It is an easy version of the classic French Ile Flotant, *also known as the Floating Island dessert. With the* Ile Flotant, *the meringue is cooked spoon by spoon into hot milk making for its lighter quality although, like the* **canonigo**, *it also has the caramel and custard sauce.*

2 tbsps. butter
1 cup sugar
1/2 cup hot water
8 egg whites
1/2 cup sugar
1 tsp. baking powder

Sauce:

1/2 cup sugar
8 yolks, slightly beaten
1 cup evaporated milk
1/4 cup rum
1 tsp. vanilla

Butter bottom and sides of two 9-inch loaf pans; set aside.
Melt 1 cup sugar in a heavy saucepan over low heat, until golden. Add water to dissolve caramelized sugar. Divide mixture in the buttered pans; set aside.
Beat egg whites until soft peaks form. Gradually add sugar beating continuously until stiff but not dry. Bake on a preheated oven at 350°F for 30 minutes or until light brown. Cool and unmold in a platter. Prepare sauce.

Sauce:
Combine first three ingredients and cook over double boiler until thick. Remove from fire and rum and vanilla. Cool and spoon over canonigo or serve seperately.

Chocolate Crinkles

Crinkles are a popular type of drop cookies. Some are light as cakes and some are chewy. Here is one easy version.

3/4 cup butter or margarine
1 cup sugar
1 cup packed brown sugar
3 eggs
1 tsp. vanilla
1 1/2 cups flour
1 cup cocoa
1/4 cup milk with 1 tsp. *calamansi* juice (to make into sour milk)
1 tbsp. baking powder
1 tsp. baking soda
Powdered sugar to sprinkle on top of crinkles

Preheat oven at 350°F.
Cream butter with the sugars. Beat in eggs, vanilla and sour milk.
Sift together the dry ingredients and blend into the creamed mixture. Drop by rounded teaspoonfuls onto a greased baking sheet and bake until done (about 13 to 15 minutes). Allow to cool in the sheets and remove when they are firm. Using a strainer, sprinkle top of crinkles with powdered sugar.

Antique Sweets

In the old days the peanut brittle was not a special food and people were apologetic for serving it and so it was also called *Dulce de Pacencia* as in "*Pasensiya na kayo at yan lang ang makakayanan namin.*"

The *Pinaso* was an even simpler dish made of carabao's milk (substituted today with evaporated milk), eggs and ground crackers, *Skyflakes* instead of *Jacobs* that the old people once used. Everything was just mixed and heated until the mixture had a thick consistency, then sugar was spread on top and burnt with hot *sianse*, hence the name *Pinaso*. **MF**

Lemon Squares

This dessert became fashionable in the Eighties. I am almost sure that this recipe originated in the United States mainly because of the use of lemon juice. Filipinos, however, have adopted it completely and today, it is a popular item in most cake shops and homes.

6 tbsp. butter or margarine
1/4 cup granulated sugar
1 cup all-purpose flour
2 eggs
3/4 cup granulated sugar
2 tbsp. all-purpose flour
1/4 tsp. finely shredded lemon peel
3 tbsp. lemon juice
1/2 tsp. baking powder
1/2 - 3/4 powdered sugar

Grease an 8x8x2-inch baking pan. Beat butter for 30 seconds; add the 1/4 cup sugar and teaspoon salt, beating till fluffy. Stir in the 1 cup flour. Pat dough onto bottom of pan. Bake in a 350°F oven for 15 minutes.

Meanwhile, beat eggs; add remaining 3/4 cup sugar, 2 tablespoons flour, lemon peel, lemon juice, and baking powder. Beat 3 minutes or till slightly thickened. Pour over baked layer. Bake in a 350°F oven 25 to 30 minutes longer till light golden brown around edges and center is set. Cool. Sift powdered sugar on top. Cut into squares. Makes 16.

Elegant Mousse Torte

This won second place in the 1979 Maya Cookfest for Fanny T. So of Quezon City

Crust:
> 3/4 cup plus 2 tbsp. Gold Medal all-purpose flour
> 3 tbsp. sugar
> 1 Maya Farms eggyolk
> 1/4 cup butter

Cake:
> 6 Maya Farm eggyolks
> 3 tbsp. lemon juice
> 1/2 tsp. lemon rind
> 1 to 3/4 cups sifted confectioners' sugar
> 6 Maya Farm egg whites
> 1 cup sifted Softasilk Cake Flour
> 1/4 cup sifted cornstarch
> 3/4 tsp baking powder
> 1/2 cup crushed pineapple
> 1/2 cup grated sweet chocolate
> 1/4 cup melted butter

Mousse Filling & Frosting:
> 1 tbsp. unflavored gelatin
> 3 tbsp. cold water
> 2 cups whipping cream
> 3/4 cup confectioners' sugar
> 1/2 cup crushed pineapple
> 1 cup grated sweet chocolate

Kirsch mixture:
> 1/4 cup water
> 2 tbsp. kirsch or rum
> 2 tbsp. sugar

Preheat oven to 350°F. Line and grease the bottoms of three 9-inch round layer pans. Set aside.

Prepare Crust:
Sift flour and sugar into a bowl; add eggyolk and butter and blend well to make a smooth dough. Roll into a circle 9 inches in diameter between two pieces of wax paper. Prick all over and chill for 30 minutes. Bake on a cookie sheet for 20 minutes or until lightly browned.

Prepare Cake:
Combine eggyolks, lemon juice, lemon rind and sugar; beat until light and creamy. In another bowl, beat eggwhites until stiff and then fold into eggyolk mixture. Sift together flour, cornstarch and baking powder and fold into egg mixture. Finally, blend in pineapple, chocolate and butter. Pour mixture into the prepared pans and bake for 12 to 15 minutes or until done.

Prepare Filling:
Soften gelatin in water for a few minutes and cook over low fire until gelatin is dissolved. Allow to cool. Whip cream until stiff and beat in cooked gelatin and confectioners' sugar. Set aside 3/4 cup for piping. Add pineapple and chocolate to the remaining whipped cream; set aside.

Blend ingredients for kirsch mixture in a cup and drizzle generously on top of cake.

To assemble torte:
Place a crust in a platter. Spread thinly with mousse filling then top with a cake layer. Repeat procedure until cake is assembled. Frost sides and top with remaining mousse frosting. Use remaining 3/4 cup whipped cream for piping borders and decorate with grated chocolate. Serves 12.

Chocolate Cream Cheese Cake

Another Maya winner is this recipe from Ana Gutierrez.

Chocolate Frosting:
    1 225-gram pack cream cheese
    3/4 cup butter
    2 1/2 tsp. vanilla
    2 tsp. orange extract
    1 450-gram confectioners' sugar
    1 tbsp. *creme de cacao*
    4 squares unsweetened chocolate, melted
    1/4 cup butter
    1/2 cup all-purpose cream

Chocolate Cake:
    2 1/4 cups Gold Medal All-Purpose Flour
    1 1/2 tsp. baking soda
    2 tbsp. confectioners' sugar, sifted
    1 tsp. salt
    1/4 cup butter
    2 cups chocolate frosting
    3 Maya Farms eggs
    3/4 cups milk
    2 tbsp. *creme de cacao*
    3/4 cup sliced maraschino cherries
    3/4 cup chopped cashew nuts
    Whole maraschino cherries

Chocolate Filling:
    1/2 cup chocolate frosting
    1/4 cup chopped cashew nuts

Preheat the oven to 350°F. Line two 9-inch round layer pans with wax paper. Set aside.

Prepare Frosting:
Cream the cream cheese and butter until soft and fluffy. Add flavoring. Blend well. Blend in confectioners' sugar gradually; add cream de cacao and melted chocolate; mix well and set 2 cups of the mixture aside for the cake. To the remaining frosting, blend in butter and

cream; get 1/2 cup of mixture for filling and add to it 1/4 cup cashew nuts. Set aside.

Prepare Cake:
Sift flour, baking soda, confectioners' sugar and salt together. Set aside.

Cream butter and 2 cups chocolate frosting. Add eggs one at a time, beating well after each addition. Add dry ingredients alternately with milk and creme de cacao. Blend well.

Fold in cherries and turn mixture into the prepared pans. Bake for 30 to 40 minutes or until done. Cool and remove from pans.

To assemble:
Place one layer of cake on a round serving plate. Spread with prepared filling. Top with another layer and ice cake decoratively with remaining frosting. Decorate sides and border of cake as desired.

Spritz Cookies

1 cup soft butter or margarine
2/3 cup sugar
3 egg yolks
1 tsp. vanilla
1 1/2 cup all-purpose flour

Mix thoroughly soft butter, sugar, egg yolks and vanilla. Work into flour with hands. Force the dough through a cookie press onto ungreased baking sheet in letter S, rosettes, fluted bars or other desired shapes. Bake until set, but not brown (about 7 to 10 minutes at 400°F.)

Mango Cake

Josefina C. Sincioco's dessert recipe won first prize in the 1983 Maya Cookfest. She is now one of the top pastry chefs in the business gaining experience in the kitchens of a five star hotel and a top-rated Metro Manila restaurant.

Cake:
 2 cups sifted Softasilk Cake Flour
 1 tbsp. baking powder
 1/2 tsp. salt
 1 cup sugar
 1 cup chilled whipping cream
 4 Maya Farms eggwhites
 1/2 tsp. cream of tartar
 1/2 cup mango juice

Cream Filling:
 1/4 cup butter
 1/4 cup cheese spread
 6 tbsp. confectioners' sugar
 1 big ripe mango, sliced

Cream Frosting:
 1.3 cup cream cheese
 1 1/2 cups whipping cream
 1 cup sifted confectioners' sugar
 2 tsp. unflavored gelatin, dissolved in
 3 tbsp. mango nectar or juice over low fire
 3 drops yellow food color

Mango Glaze:
 1.4 cup confectioners' sugar
 2 tsp. cornstarch
 1/2 cup mango juice or nectar
 10 drops yellow food color

Garnishing:
 Mango slices
 Mango preserves
 Tinted *kaong* (sugar palm)

Preheat oven to 350°F. Line two 9-inch layer pans. Set aside.

Sift together flour, baking powder, salt and sugar into a bowl. Set aside.

With chilled bowl and beater over another bowl of ice water, beat whipping cream until soft peaks form. Beat in 1/4 of the sugar and continue beating stiff. Refrigerate.

Beat eggwhites with cream of tartar until frothy. Add remaining sugar and beat until stiff peaks form. Fold in whipped cream then the dry ingredients alternately with mango juice into cream mixture. Blend well. Pour in prepared pans and bake for 30 to 35 minutes or until done. Let cool in pans for 10 minutes then remove from pan. Let cool completely on wire racks.

Prepare Cream Frosting:

Beat cream cheese until soft and creamy. Add whipping cream and beat until thick. Gradually add sugar, beating continuously until stiff. Beat in gelatin mixture and coloring. Set aside in refrigerator.

Prepare Cream Filling:

Cream butter and cheese spread until soft. Add sugar and continue beating until well-blended. Add 1/2 cup of the cream frosting and beat into butter mixture. Fold in sliced mangoes. Set aside.

Prepare Mango Glaze:

Combine all ingredients and cook, stirring continuously over low fire until mixture thickens. Allow to cool.

To assemble cake:

Spread mango glaze on top of each cake layer. Place one layer on a serving platter then spread cream filling. Top with other layer then frost top and sides decoratively with cream frosting. Decorate with mango preserves and tinted kaong. Drizzle remaining glaze on cake, allowing it to drip down the sides. Chill.

Frittata

Pizza is a part of our cuisine now. Other Italian food in the pastas have become a regular feature in most restaurants today. But there is another Italian dish that is as terrific yet is not that known. Margarita Fores, one of our young chefs who trained in Italy, shared this frittata recipe with me on my TV show.

At one of my dinners in Paris, I decided to serve Margarita's recipe. I remembered the flavor and the fact that it was mainly made up of leftovers. What daunted me was that I knew I could not flip the frittata as expertly as Margarita did. So I bought two non-stick frying pans, one to cook one side of the frittata and when done take the other frying pan over it, flip the two pans and cook the other side on the other frying pan. That ought to be a good tip to those who, like me, are intimidated about not being expert frittata flippers.

10 eggs
1/2 cup cream
1/4 tsp. salt
1/8 tsp. pepper
1 tbsp. vegetable oil

Filling:
6 slices cooked bacon or 1/2 cup cooked ham, diced or cut into small pieces
1/3 cup cheddar cheese, in cubes
1 cup cooked pasta
1/2 cup cooked meats (chicken, pork, or beef)
1 green or red sweet pepper, diced
1/4 cup Swiss Cheese
1/3 cup coarsely grated Parmessan Cheese
8 to 10 pieces of green or black olives (optional)

Prepare filling. Blend eggs, cream, salt and pepper. Heat oil in an 8-inch oven-proof skillet. Pour egg mixture into skillet; cook over medium-low heat. As eggs set, run spatula around edge, lifting to allow uncooked egg to flow underneath. Arrange filling on top. Cook until almost all is set but surface is moist. Instead of flipping, the frittata may be placed in the oven and broiled 4 inches from the heat until top is set (from 2 to 3 minutes). Serve immediately.

ILOILO

GABI WITH SNAILS
PORK WITH KADIOS & JACKFRUIT
MANGARACHADA
CHICKEN WITH KADIOS & UBAD
PANCIT MOLO
GINATANG TAMBO WITH ALIMASAG

To LEARN more about the cuisine of Iloilo, I flew south to visit with some of the city's food experts. These were Maridel Padilla, Rosalie Sarabia Trenas, Cora Lavaro, Teresita Sanson Larraga of the famous Panaderia de Molo and my hosts, Jessie and Arlette Ledesma of the Hotel del Rio.

Baby Sanson Larraga gave me a glimpse of her kitchen while Arlette Ledesma and I worked in hers. Cora Lavaro of the Casa Plaza Hotel, on the other hand, took me to the wet market at 6 in the morning.

The market trip yielded one of bagongon, a cone-shaped mollusk, which Cora cooked with gabi and coconut milk flavored with guinamus, a paste of tiny shrimps. A similar dish of gabi with snails is included here which also includes a detailed description of Cora's technique in cooking the bagongon, a big help for those who would like to know how to cook coconut milk just right.

Maridel and Delia Padilla demonstrated a dish of preserved fish eggs called bihud which is not among the recipes but which is simple enough to learn. The bihud is sauted in garlic, onions and tomatoes. The bihud is then served two ways. One part still has a bit of sauce. The other is cooked until all the juices evaporate, and then some oil is added and the bihud is cooked until crisp.

But it was in Arlette Ledesma's well-equipped kitchen where Arlette, her chef and I tested the recipes here, a sampling of food as prepared in Iloilo. We took all afternoon to try each dish and measure the ingredients used. All the recipes here are from Arlette especially the Manga-rachada which she so generously shared with us considering that she sells the pickled mangoes she makes.

In Arlette's Pancit Molo recipe, the strong Chinese influence is there since the dish uses tahure and kutsay. My own Pancit Molo recipe compiled more than 20 years ago did not have these ingredients.

Also included in this Iloilo collection is the kadios with chicken and ubad (pith of the banana tree), a favorite dish there. Ilonggos pine for this as well as guinamos and muscovado when they are far away from home. Those of you who long for Ilonggo cooking will find Arlette's recipes good, practical and authentic.

Kaon kamo sing maayo!

Cora Lavaro's Gabi with Bagongon

1 cup *gabi* tuber and root, peeled and cut up
2 cups *gabi* stalks, cut into half inch slices
15 pcs. snails
2 tbsp. *bagongon* (*guinamus*), mixed with 2 tbsp. water
1 1/2 cup *gata* (coconut cream, first extract)

Cora began by sauteing her *guinamus* (preserved shrimp paste) in ginger. To this she added the roots, tuber, stalks and leaves of *gabi*. With just enough water to cook the gabi and *bagongon* (a cone-shaped snail mollusk), she waited until every ingredient was cooked just right then she added the coconut cream. This was the crucial part. The coconut cream was simmered gently for a short period. The result was a perfectly balanced dish with just the right flavor and the coconut cream rich and uncurdled.

Pork with Kadios & Jackfruit

1/4 kilo pork, cut into pieces
1 cup *kadios*
4 cups chicken stock
2 cups young jackfruit (*langka*), sliced thinly
2 tbsp. cooking oil
1/2 head garlic, crushed and chopped
1 pc. onion, sliced
2 pcs. tomatoes, cubed
1 cup *malunggay* leaves
1 tbsp. rock salt
1/2 tsp. msg

Saute garlic, onions, tomatoes. Drop in pork slices and *kadios*. Add chicken stock and boil till pork pieces are soft. Then add jackfruit slices. Season with rock salt and msg. When pork and jackfruit slices are tender, drop in *malunggay* leaves. Cover and let cook for 1 minute. Remove from fire. Serve hot.

Mangarachada (Pickled Mangoes)

10 pcs. green mangoes (very green)
1 cup salt
3 cups vinegar
1 1/2 cups sugar
1 head garlic (crushed)

Cut the green mangoes into half. Remove all parts of the seed. Sprinkle with salt generously. Arrange the mango halves in a container with skin side up. Allow to soak in salt overnight.

The next day, wash mangoes in running water. Arrange mangoes once more in the container with skin side up. Pour in vinegar mixture (3 cups vinegar and 1 1/2 cups sugar) and cover. After a day, it will be ready to serve.

To serve, cut mango halves into bite-size pieces.

Chicken with Kadios & Ubad

Kadios *is a black-eyed bean which is also called pigeon pea while* ubad *is the heart of the banana stalk. Both are favorites of Ilonggos. The* ubad, *according to food writer Edilberto Alegre, is also called "flourescent" in that region probably because it resembles the long thin flourscent light.* **MF**

1/2 of a chicken (500 gms.), cut into pieces
2 pcs. *ubad* (banana tree core)
1 cup *kadios*, fresh
2 pcs. tomatoes, sliced
1 pc. onion, sliced
1/2 head garlic, peeled and sliced thinly
1 tbsp. margarine
1 stalk *tanglad* (lemon grass), bundled
2 cups chicken stock
1 stalk green onions, cut into small pieces
1 tsp. rock salt
1/4 tsp. msg

Slice the *ubad* thinly. Sprinkle with rock salt and squeeze, removing the sap. Wash with water and squeeze dry. Makes approximately 2 cups.

Saute garlic, tomatoes, and onions in margarine. Cover to cook. Then drop in chicken pieces, *ubad, kadios* and *tanglad.* Season with rock salt and msg.

Add chicken stock and boil until chicken pieces are tender. Correct seasoning and serve.

Pancit Molo

Right after the Second World War, Mrs. Conchita Visplana made a name for herself with her delicious **Pancit Molo**. *Most of Manila's society sampled her good cooking. Apart from* Pancit Molo, *she sold fresh* lumpia *and* dinuguan *by the ton (almost). Since her specialties were always impeccable and the making of the dishes she sold were a mystery to many at that time, she cornered and, perhaps, unwittingly started "take out" service in Manila. I never got to ask her for her recipe but here is a very good version of* Pancit Molo *which an Ilongga showed me right in her kitchen.*

Arlette Deles Ledesma re-introduced Pancit Molo *to me. We both tested this recipe in her kitchen in Iloilo, the province where the town of Molo is, and from where the dish originated. I told her that her version is the nearest to the original. Arlette is food and beverage manager of Hotel Del Rio in Iloilo City.*

50 pcs. *molo* wrapper
1/4 k. ground pork
1 egg, sligthly beaten
1/2 cube *tahure* (mashed)
1 stalk *kutsay* leaves, cut into small pieces
1/2 tsp. soy sauce
1/4 tsp. msg
1/4 tsp. ground black pepper
3 tbsp. margarine
3 cloves garlic
100 gms. shrimp, peeled, boiled and cut up
1/4 pc. chicken, boiled and cut up into small pieces
4 cups chicken broth
rock salt
2 stalks green onion, cut finely

Mix ground pork, half the beaten egg, *tahure*, *kutsay*, soy sauce, msg and pepper. To make *molo* heads, oil 1/2 tsp. of the mixture in one corner of the square wrapper and seal using the remaining egg and 1 tsp. flour mixture.

Saute 4 cloves of garlic in 1 tbsp. of margarine until golden brown. Add in shrimps and chicken pieces. Add in 4 cups chicken broth. Season with rock salt to taste. Drop in the *molo* heads one by one. Cover and cook for about 3 minutes only so wrapper won't be over-cooked. Drop into 2 stalks of onion leaves and sprinkle a dash of pepper. Remove from fire. Serve hot.

Ginatang Tambo with Alimasag

2 cups *tambo* (fresh bamboo shoots), sliced thinly [These come from farms and mountains of Iloilo]
2 cups water
1/2 cup young corn, grated
1 cup *tugabang* leaves (saluyot), cut up
2 pcs. *alimasag*
4 pcs. okra, cut in three
2 tbsp. *guinamus* (*bagoong*) mixed with 2 tbsp. water
1/2 tbsp. salt
1/2 cup *gata* (coconut cream, first extract)
1/2 cup *gata* (coconut cream, second extract)

Blanch *tambo*. Squeeze dry. Add in *guinamus* mixture, *alimasag* and grated corn and okra. Boil with 2 cups water. Add *tugabang* leaves. Let cook until *tambo* is soft. Add second extract coconut cream. Season with salt. After 2 minutes, drop in first extract of coconut cream. Allow to simmer gently for 2 minutes and serve.

Pancit Malabon

There are many versions of the pancit Malabon. The Pascual family of that town serve the noodles, called *bihon sariwa*, and the mixtures, called *sahog*, separate. There would be two kilos of fresh shrimps, the dark variety called *swahe*, still jumping when bought. There would be pork cubes, *tinapa* (smoked fish) that was just bought and then shredded, newly cooked *chicharon* which was pounded to bits, and sliced native *pechay*.

It is the sauce, called the *palabok*, which distinguishes one pancit Malabon from another. The sauce is all-important which is why the noodle dish is also known as *pancit palabok*. The sauce is usually made of shrimp stock, a dozen egg yolks, a little bit of *achuete*, some starch for a thicker consistency, and of course, the best *patis* and some *calamansi* for flavoring.

The old way Pancit Malabon was made was quite different. It had no *palabok*, just the *sahog*, the noodles cooked with oil from pork fat and colored with *achuete*. In the old days also, the *luglug* was eaten in a small soup bowl called a *mangkok*, the kind the Chinese use as rice bowl. These days, the *pancit* is almost always served in bigger Western style soup bowls. The bowl may be all that remains of the Chinese influence because there used to be a time when the *pancit* was eaten with bamboo chopsticks they called "*sipit*." Another surprising trivia was a side dish known as *balubad* that was supposed to neutralize the taste of the rich *palabok* sauce or as the Tagalogs would put it, "*pampaalis ng suya*." It was doubly surprising to find out that *balubad* is the yellow fruit of the *casuy*.

Pancit luglug is another name for pancit Malabon because the noodles are dipped with a bamboo strainer into boiling stock and the action is called "*niluluglug*." The *luglug* is usually eaten with *kamachile* cookies, a dry kind of cookie with a slight buttery taste so called because it is shaped like the *kamachile* fruit. **MF**

KAKANIN

BIBINGKANG GALAPONG
BIKO
PALITAO
CASSAVA BIBINGKA
CUCHINTA
ESPASOL
GULA MELAKA
ALING ZENY'S GUINATAAN
HALO-HALO
MARUYA
PICHI-PICHI
PINTOS
SPECIAL POLVORON WITH CRISP
PINIPIG
PUTO
TINAPAY SAN NICOLAS
TINUTONG
SAPIN-SAPIN

K**AKANIN** *IS one phase of Philippine cuisine I am uncomfortable with.
My own recollection of* kakanin *is limited to the* bibingkang galap̄-
ong, suman sa lijia, polvoron *and* espasol. *And what I do remember of
them was bought from* manlalako, *a food vender who carried wares in
covered baskets who shout out the name of the* kakanin *being sold. The
sight of the* puto-kuchinta *vender is common in our streets, a man who
balances two round metal containers on each end of a bamboo pole.
Inside the containers are white hot* puto *on one side and red-orange*
kuchinta *on the other. Both come with freshly grated coconut.*

*One can go to any wet market in the country and there will be an
assortment of rice cakes, rice puddings,* camote *sweets, banana cues,*
guinataan, maruya, sapin-sapin, *a variety of* bibingka, *and* kalamay *all
using what one finds all over the islands: plain or glutinous rice (*malagkit*); tubers such as* gabi, ubi, camote *in all variations; corn as in the*
binatog; *plus the coconut, our tree of life, in its various stages, from the
young* buko *to the mature* niyog.

When you say bibingka, *you have to specify the kind*—galapong,
kanin, mais, kamoteng kahoy, malagkit.

Guinataan *also comes in various versions*—mais, mongo *or* tinutong,
saging *and a combination of many ingredients, the* halo-halo.
Everytime I was given guinataang halo-halo, *I used to scoop out the*
malagkit *ball first because it was a favorite. Now there is a* guinataan
that contains nothing but malagkit balls, *called* bilo-bilo.

Bibingkang Galapong

2 cups rice (*laon*), soaked in water enough to cover for 4 - 8 hours
1 tbsp. fermented *galapong* or *libadora*
2 cups water
1 cup sugar
1/2 tsp. baking soda
3/4 cup water
1 egg, beaten
baking powder
sugar

Toppings:
sliced cheese
sliced red eggs (*itlog na maalat*)

Add fermented *galapong* or *libadora* and 2 cups water to the soaked rice and pass through a blender until mixture is thick and smooth. Stir in sugar and baking soda.

Measure 1 cup of the thick *galapong* mixture and dilute with 3/4 cup of water. Add the beaten egg. Set aside.

Prepare 10 cm. (4") round clay pot* lined with banana leaves. Get about 1/4 cup of the diluted mixture and add 1/4 tsp. baking powder and 1 tbsp. sugar. Pour into prepared clay pot. Garnish with cheese and red eggs. Bake or cook using charcoal until done. Repeat procedure.

* Clay pot can be bought in some wet markets, dry goods section.

Biko

5 cups (1 kilo) glutinous rice (*malagkit*)
5 cups water
4 cups thick coconut milk
3 cups brown sugar
1/2 tsp. salt
1/2 tsp. anise seeds

Wash *malagkit* in a pot. Add water and boil until done. In a big carajay, combine the remaining ingredients; mix well and boil until thick. Lower heat and add the cooked *malagkit*. Blend well and continue cooking, stirring constantly until mixture is very thick and heavy to handle. Remove from fire and transfer to a platter or form into small mounds. Arrange mounds in a plate lined with banana leaf.

Note: To vary flavor, omit anise seeds and add 1 small piece ginger, crushed. Discard ginger before serving.

Palitao

In the old days, we used to soak the malagkit *rice and then grind it in the stone* gilingan *(grinder). Then the ground* malagkit *was tied in a* katcha *and allowed to hang so that the excess water was drained out. Today, one can get the* giniling na malagkit *ready-made in any wet market. Abroad, many Oriental stores carry the sticky rice flour.*

2 cups sticky rice flour
2/3 cup water
pinch of salt
6 to 8 cups boiling water
2 cups fresh, grated coconut
1 cup toasted sesame seeds *
2 cups sugar

Dissolve the pinch of salt in the 2/3 cup water. Add the sticky rice flour and form into flat oval-shaped pieces (about 2 1/2 inches long). Set aside. Boil water in a wide mouthed pan and drop the sticky rice ovals. When the dough floats, the *palitao* is cooked. Remove the cooked *palitao* and coat it with grated coconut. Sprinkle it with a mixture of toasted sesame seeds and sugar. You may want to serve some sugar and toasted sesame on the side.

*Toast sesame seeds by spreading these on a cookie sheet and toasting in the oven until slightly brown. Or the sesame seeds can be browned in a warm pan. Stir constantly to prevent the sesame from burning.

Cassava Bibingka

This is a slight modification of a recipe I learned from Nena Zafra, an active member of the Homemakers Club of the Philippines.

2 cups grated fresh cassava
2 tbsp. margarine, melted
1 cup sugar
2 eggs, beaten
1 cup coconut milk

Mix all ingredients together and blend well. Line a pie plate of *bibingka* mold with banana leaves that have been wilted.* Pour mixture into the lined pan and bake for 30 - 35 minutes in an oven at 350°F.

Topping:

1/2 cup evaporated milk
1/2 cup thick coconut milk
2 tbsp. sugar
2 tbsp. flour
1 egg yolk, slightly beaten

Mix evaporated milk, coconut milk, flour and sugar in a pan. Cook over slow flame until mixture thickens but be sure to stir continuously. When mixture is thick, add the beaten egg yolk and cook for 2 minutes more. Spread on top of the baked cassava *bibingka*. Broil at 400°F for 10 minutes or until golden brown.

Cuchinta

1 cup rice
1 cup water
1 cup sugar
1 cup *lijia**

Soak overnight 1 cup rice with 1 cup water. Next day, grind the soaked rice fine. To this add 1 cup sugar and 1 cup *lijia*. Mix well and place in small cups and steam from 10 - 20 minutes.

Espasol

This is one Filipino dessert that will always remind me of my grand-mother, Cresenciana de los Reyes Villanueva. We were in her spacious kitchen preparing for her delicious Bibingka Galapong *when she wanted to tell me about another dessert she liked but could not remember the name. "Sol... sup... sul...", she said as she groped for the word. When she finally got it, she laughed in triumph and said, "***Espasol!***"*

This recipe is a simpler way to make this delicious dessert. It will serve about 20 persons and the espasol can keep for about 5 days.

3 cups glutinous rice (*malagkit*) flour
2 cups coconut cream
2 1/2 cups sugar
1 1/4 cups grated young coconut (*buko*)

Toast rice flour over low fire until light brown. Set aside.

Bring coconut cream to boil. Add sugar and stir continuously for 15 minutes. Blend in young coconut and toasted rice flour, reserving 1/2 cup flour for dusting. Continue cooking over low fire until mixture is thick. Let cool for a while.

Line a tray with greaseproof paper and dust with the reserved rice flour. Spread mixture onto tray and flatten to about 1 inch thick. Cut into 3 cm. x 10 cm. bars.

Coat each piece with toasted rice flour. Wrap in colored cellophane. The *espasol* will keep for only a day or two.

Gula Melaka
(Sago dessert with palm and coconut milk)

Much loved by the colonial British, this is still a favorite dessert after an expansive curry tiffin (lunch).

2 cups pearl sago
6 - 8 cups boiling water
1 tbsp. milk
1 cup thick coconut milk
pinch salt

Syrup:
250 gms. (8 oz) palm sugar (*gula Melaka*) or
200 gms (6 1/2 oz) brown sugar with 2 tbsp. treacle (molasses)
1 1/2 cups water
1 *pandan* leaf (optional)

Put sago in sieve and pick over to remove any grit or foreign matter. Shake the sieve to dislodge any dust but do not wash sago or it will become gluey. Fill a very large saucepan with boiling water. When it is boiling rapidly, pour the sago into the pan in a thin stream, stirring all the time with a wooden spoon. Boil about 10 minutes, stirring constantly until balls of *sago* swell and become transparent. Pour sago into a large sieve and hold running water to wash away the starch. Shake the sieve until all the liquid has gone. Stir in milk to give sago a white color, then put sago into a large mold or into 8 - 10 small molds. Cool, then refrigerate until needed.

Put coconut milk in a jug and stir in salt. Store in refrigerator.

To make syrup, put palm sugar or brown sugar with treacle in a pan. If using *pandan* leaf, scrape with a fork, tie into a bundle then place in the pan. Add water to pan. Simmer until sugar has dissolved, then continue cooking until syrup has reduced to about one cup. Sieve then discard *pandan* leaf. Put syrup into a jug and leave to cool.

When serving, unmold the *sago* and pour a little coconut milk and syrup over each individual serving.

Aling Zeny's Guinataan Halo-halo

Aling Zeny (Azucena Balaoro) has been our family cook for ages. She is a natural cook. Her "timpla" palate balances flavors just right and her cooking has gained the approval of waiters, employees and even our cooks at the Au Bon Vivant.

Aling Zeny did not want to give all her secrets in the preparation of her guinataan at first, but in the interest of having good Filipino food enjoyed by others, she has parted with her secrets. This guinataan recipe is served whenever anyone of us has a birthday.

(good for 40 - 50 persons)

5 - 6 mature coconuts (*niyog*), grated
1/4 kilo *sago* (tapioca balls, large size)
1/4 kilo ripe jackfruit (*langka*) in strips
4 leaves of *pandan* (screwpine leaves)
1/4 kilo *ube* (violet yam)
1 kilo *gabi* (taro)
1 kilo *camote* (sweet potato)
15 pcs. *saba* banana (adding more will make the *guinataan* slightly sour)
1 kilo *galapong malagkit* (glutinous rice flour with enough water to make a sticky ball. This is sold in wet markets.), shape into marble-size balls.
1 kilo sugar

Peel all tubers and cut into bite-size pieces. Keep them in separate mounds as they take different lengths of time to cook.[*]

Boil 2 cups of water and drop *sago* to cook. Set aside in cold water. Add 3 cups of warm water to the grated coconut and put this into a cheesecloth. Squeeze out the coconut cream. Set aside. Add 20 cups of water to the grated coconut and squeeze out all the liquid. It should yield about 25 cups of thin coconut milk. Strain.

In a large saucepan, mix the coconut milk and sugar and allow this to boil. Add *sago*, *langka* strips and *pandan* leaves to give the coconut milk a nice flavor and aroma. Add *ube*. After 5 minutes, add *gabi*. After 5 minutes add the *camote*. After 3 minutes, add the *saba* banana. After two minutes add the *galapong* balls. When the balls rise to the top, they are cooked. Shut off the flame. Now, add the thick coconut cream.

Add the sugar, first half a kilo, then add little by little according to how sweet you want the *guinataan*. A few grains of salt will improve the flavor. Remove *pandan* leaves and serve in bowls or cups.

* Note: It is important to cut the tubers so that one can savor each piece. The tubers should be added to the boiling coconut milk depending on the time it takes for each kind of tuber to be cooked so that all of them will be cooked by the time the last one is done. The timing suggested here is an approximation. Practice, however, makes perfect but bear in mind that the intensity of heat (low, medium, high) you use in cooking does determine the length of cooking time.

Maruya

1 cup sifted all-purpose flour
1 tsp. baking powder
1 tsp. salt
2 eggs
1/2 cup milk
1 tsp. melted fat or vegetable lard
***saba* bananas, sliced lengthwise**

Sift dry ingredients into a bowl. Set aside.
Mix eggs, milk and oil. Add to dry ingredients. Beat until smooth. Dip *saba* in batter and deep-fat fry. Drain on absorbent paper. Roll in sugar.

Variation:
Sweet *camote* (sliced thinly) may be used instead of *saba* bananas,

Pichi-pichi

1 cup *camoteng kahoy*, grated
1 cup sugar
2 cups water
1 grated coconut (*niyog*)

Squeeze the *camoteng kahoy* to remove the juice. Put the squeezed *camoteng kahoy* in a pan and add the sugar and water. Cook while stirring continuously for around 10 minutes or until the mixture coats the spoon. Put cooked mixture on individual muffin pans and steam for about 10 minutes. Remove from pans and roll in grated coconut.

Pintos
(Cebu corn pudding)

2 cups scraped young corn (from fresh young corn on the cob)
3/4 cup scraped *buko* (young coconut meat)
1 can condensed milk
2 egg yolks
2 tbsp. butter, melted
1/4 cup cornstarch

Mix all the ingredients in a bowl. Prepare fresh husk of the young corn. (The husk near the cob is best as it is more pliable and easier to handle.) Drop a heaping tablespoon of the young corn mixture into the middle of the corn husk. One can either roll the husk lengthwise and tie the ends or bring the two ends together, tie them then push the mixture to the center. (see diagram)

Select a saucepan so that the size will hold the scraped corn cobs. Cut the corn cobs and arranged them at the bottom of a saucepan so that they create a bed for the *pintos*. Add water to saucepan making sure that the water does not reach the corn mixture or this will dilute the *pintos* and ruin the pudding. Steam for about 20 minutes. The flavor of the corn cob will dissolve in the water and will add flavor to the *pintos*.

Special Polvoron with Crisp Pinipig

1/2 cup cooking oil
1/2 cup *pinipig*
1 1/2 cups cake flour
3/4 cup powdered milk
1/2 cup melted butter
3/4 cup sugar

Heat cooking oil in a pan and fry the *pinipig*. Set aside.

Heat a skillet and brown the flour until light golden brown in color (around 5 - 10 minutes). Add powdered milk and toss for another 2 minutes. Add sugar, melted butter and fried *pinipig*. Blend well. Mold and wrap in Japanese paper.

Puto

1/4 cup shortening
3 tbsp. sugar
1 cup flour
1 tsp. baking powder
1/8 tsp. salt
6 tbsp. milk (a little over 1/3 cup)
4 egg whites
2 tbsp. sugar

Cream shortening and add 3 tbsp. sugar. Sift dry ingredients together. Add 6 tbsp. milk and sifted dry ingredients alternately to shortening and sugar mixture. Set aside.

Beat egg whites until stiff. Add 2 tbsp. sugar (this helps keep the air in the beaten egg whites). Fold the egg whites into the mixture. Pour into muffin pans. Steam for about 20 minutes or until done. Serve hot or cold.

Note: A few anise seeds sprinkled on puto adds flavor.

Tibok-tibok

In Angeles, Pampanga, there is this immaculate white sweetness called **tibok-tibok**, so named because any movement causes the concoction to imitate heartbeat vibrations. It is really *maja blanca* made of carabao's milk, with toasted *latik* strewn on top. One variation has corn bits.

Puto

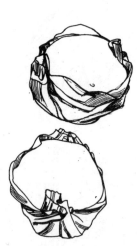

The Manapla **puto** is named after the town in Iloilo known for this type of *puto*. It is almost round in shape with an underliner made of banana leaf. The leaf has to come only from the *saba* variety because the *latundan* leaf gives off a bitter taste. Only old rice can be used since new rice tends to be too sticky. The Manapla *puto* is usually paired with the *batchòy* but is great by itself.

An expert *puto*-maker considers *puto*-making a more delicate procedure than baking a cake. The weather makes a lot of difference. If it's too hot, fermentation is faster and the *puto* might taste a bit sour. If it's too cold, the mixture might not rise. Shelf life is only for one day but with freezing, the *puto* can last for one week.

Suman sa Leyte

Fiesta time in Leyte is also the time to look forward to tasting a variety of *suman*. It's always nice to know that you can choose from the purple *suman nga matamis* (sweetened) or the white *suman inasin* (salty). Or both can be combined as one *suman* called *tinipá* which means "cut in half", because the *suman* has a clear demarcation in color and taste, one side sweet and one side salty.

Leyte also has its variation of *suman latik* which is glutinous rice treated with lye to give it a green hue and then sweetened with *latik* after cooking. The difference with other regions is the leaves used in wrapping, not the usual banana leaf but a broad leaf they call *hagikhik*. No other leaf will do and some fiestas have done without the *suman latik* because there was no supply of *hagikhik*.

A smoother variety of *suman* is called *morón*. This is because it is made of ground glutinous rice. *Morón* is either plain or mixed with chocolate. When the two flavors are mixed in one *suman*, not in the style of the *tinipá* but swirled producing streaks of colors, its is called rainbow *morón*. Also smooth in texture is *sagmani* or *ira-id*, made of either *balanghoy* (*kamoteng kahoy*) or *gabi*, its center more sweet because it is mixed with more sugar.

The *binagól* is grated *gabi* mixed with coconut milk and sugar and then packaged in a half coconut shell, a specialty of the town of Dagami.

Tinapay San Nicolas

3 tbsp. butter
1 cup sugar
4 egg yolks
1 1/2 cups flour
1 1/2 cups corn starch
1 tbsp. baking powder
a few grains of anise
1/2 cup coconut cream

Cream butter and add sugar gradually. Beat egg yolks then incorporate into butter-sugar mixture. Using a sifter, add half of the dry ingredients to the mixture and add the coconut cream gradually. Finally add the remaining half of the dry ingredients. Mix well to create a dough.

Knead the dough on a floured table top. Roll it out with a rolling pin that has been dusted with flour until the dough is spread thinly. Cut into pieces with a cookie cutter and bake in a greased baking sheet. Brush the cookies with milk and bake in the oven at 350°F for 10 minutes.

Tinutong

This is a favorite merienda. In fact, my uncle, Dr. Jose de los Santos, liked this so much he was nicknamed "Totong."

1/4 cup mongo beans
2 cups glutinous rice (*malagkit*)
2 mature coconuts (*niyog*), grated
1 1/2 cups sugar

Toast mongo beans by cooking it in a heavy pan or kawali. Cook till mongo is golden brown. The skin of the mongo beans can then be easily peeled off. Remove skin.

Soak glutinous rice in water until the grains swell. Mix rice with toasted mongo beans.

Prepare coconut milk. Add 1 cup of warm water to grated coconut. Squeeze out coconut cream and set aside. Add 6 cups of warm water and extract coconut milk from the grated coconut. Strain the coconut milk and coconut cream, separately. Add sugar to the coconut milk and cook glutinous rice and mongo beans. Stir occasionally until mixture is done. Remove from fire and add the coconut cream. Adjust sugar. Salt may be added if desired. Serve.

Sapin-sapin

5 cups *galapong* (glutinous rice that is ground then added with water to form a sticky ball)
3 cups white sugar
1/2 tsp. annatto seeds (*achuete*) soaked in 2 tsps. water
2 cups thick coconut milk (first extraction)

Divide the *galapong* into two parts. For the first half, add 1 cup coconut milk and 1 1/2 cups sugar. Pour this into a cloth-lined (cheese cloth) container and place over a bamboo steamer. Put the steamer over a *carajay* half-filled with boiling water. Steam for about 5 minutes.

Mix the second half of the *galapong* with the annatto seed water (now colored red). Pour this over the cooked *galapong*. Steam again until done.

For variety, sweet *ube* mixture cooked in syrup may be placed as third layer.

Makes 6 - 8 servings.

INDEX